TALKABOUT Sex and Relationsh

TALKABOUT Sex & Relationships 2 is a comprehensive toolkit for all therapists, educators and support staff who deliver sex education to people with special needs. It is intended primarily to support groupwork but activities can be easily adapted to suit the needs of individuals with varying abilities.

The resource emphasises the importance of being well informed in regards to the physical, interpersonal and emotional aspects of sex; including body awareness, consent, sexual health and guidelines for a healthy sexual relationship. It is packed with practical activities which are designed to open up discussion around sensitive issues in a fun, informative and non-judgemental way. Each activity comes with guidance for practitioners on how to prepare for and deliver the sessions.

Features include:

- guidelines to assess the suitability of students for the programme
- visually appealing and engaging activities with full colour illustrations
- photocopiable activities which can also be downloaded for free on the accompanying website
- template letters for parental permission in delivering the sessions

This toolkit is the second in a two volume set, the first of which focuses on relationships. Created by Alex Kelly and Emily Dennis as part of the bestselling *Talkabout* series, this publication constitutes the most complete and trustworthy set of resources available for groupwork focussing on sex and relationships for people with special needs.

Alex Kelly is a Speech and Language Therapist who specialises in supporting people who have difficulties with their social skills, self-esteem and relationships skills. She currently runs her own business providing speech therapy, a day service for adults with autism and social skills training and consultancy to schools and organisations across the UK and overseas. She is best known as the author of the hugely popular Talkabout resources.

Emily Dennis has worked in learning disability since 2008 in a variety of settings: residential, supported living, day services and special education. Within these she worked as a Communication Coordinator delivering training and implementing communication systems across Hampshire. This included projects around service user empowerment, enabling vulnerable adults to assertively make clear and informed choices about their lives. At university Emily studied BSc (Hons) Social Care Studies and specialised in learning disability and relationships. This led her to see the need for good quality, accessible sex education and become passionate about creating a programme that would enable this. Emily worked for Alex Kelly Ltd from 2015-2018 as a project lead in sex and relationships. Their first book 'Talkabout Sex and Relationships 1' was published in 2017.

MORE BRILLIANT PROFESSIONAL RESOURCES FROM BESTSELLING AUTHOR ALEX KELLY!

TALKABOUT

Each practical workbook in this bestselling series provides a clear programme of activities designed to improve self-awareness, self-esteem and social skills.

"All in all, Alex, what a wonderful world for kids it would be if your social skills programme were in all schools across the continents"- Catherine Varapodio Longley, Parent, Melbourne, 2013.

"I feel very lucky to work in a school where our pupils get the opportunity to utilise Talkabout resources and to see the benefit that this has made to them and their peers. You are making a difference!" – Nicole Thomas, Teacher, 2017

Title	Focus	Age-range
Talkabout (2nd edition)	Developing Social Skills for all ages	7+
Talkabout for Children 1 (2nd edition)	Developing Self-Awareness and Self-Esteem	4-11
Talkabout for Children 2 (2nd edition)	Developing Social Skills	4-11
Talkabout for Children 3 (2nd edition)	Developing Friendship Skills	4-11
Talkabout for Teenagers (2nd edition)	Developing Social and Emotional Communication Skills	11-19
Talkabout for Adults	Developing Self-awareness and Self-esteem in adults	16+
Talkabout Sex and Relationships 1	Developing Intimate Relationship Skills	11+
Talkabout Sex and Relationships 2	Sex Education	11+

Also coming soon by Alex Kelly...

Social Skills: The Theory and Development of Interpersonal Communication

Bestselling author and Speech and Language Therapist Alex Kelly draws on up-to-date theory as well as her years of practical experience to bring you a definitive overview of how social skills develop, what can go wrong, and how people with social difficulties can be supported.

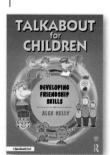
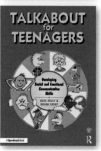
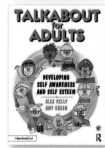
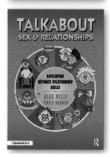

TALKABOUT
Sex and Relationships 2

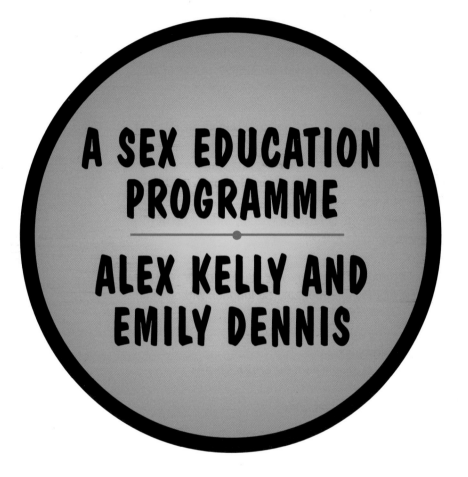

A SEX EDUCATION PROGRAMME

ALEX KELLY AND EMILY DENNIS

Routledge
Taylor & Francis Group

LONDON AND NEW YORK

First published 2019
by Routledge
2 Park Square, Milton Park, Abingdon, Oxon OX14 4RN

and by Routledge
711 Third Avenue, New York, NY 10017

Routledge is an imprint of the Taylor & Francis Group, an informa business

British Library Cataloguing-in-Publication Data
A catalogue record for this book is available from the British Library

Library of Congress Cataloging-in-Publication Data
A catalog record for this title has been requested

ISBN: 978-1-911186-21-2 (pbk)
ISBN: 978-1-315-17319-1 (ebk)

Typeset in Flora
by Apex CoVantage, LLC

Visit the companion website: http://www.routledgetextbooks.com/
textbooks/9781911186212

Contents   Page

Topic 1   Working Together

Topic 2   Body awareness

Topic 3   Let's talk about sex

Topic 4   Sex rules

Topic 5   Sex aware

Acknowledgements

We would like to thank the following people for supporting us to write this book:

Amy Green – yet again we have to thank you for your support in bringing this book together; we couldn't have done it without you.

We would also like to thank everyone at Speaking Space; you continue to be an inspiration to us and we feel privileged to be part of your journey to independence. Thank you also for being part of the pilot for this resource and your valuable feedback.

Finally we would like to mention our work colleagues who are all so lovely and supportive: Hannah Anderson, Joley Anderson, Katie Andrews, Grace Anstey, Zara Baillie, Ali Banham, Alice Caithness, Lisa Davidson, Marnie Daws, Abby Goodrich, Amy Green, Natalie Hamilton, Amy Keable, Chris Mcloughlin, Abbie Michael, Marleen Mohanlal, Alec Morley, Naomi Pearson, Brian Sains, Helen Saunt, Marina Trivett, Emily Tully, Anne Waggott and Katherine Wareham. We believe we are truly making a difference in everything we do and we want to thank you all for your enthusiasm, dedication and hard work.

This book is dedicated to everyone at Speaking Space.

About the authors

Alex Kelly is a Speech and Language Therapist with over 30 years' experience of working with both children and adults with an intellectual disability (learning disability), and specialising in working with people who have difficulties with social skills. She runs her own business (Alex Kelly Ltd) with her husband Brian Sains and is the author of a number of books and resources, including the best-selling TALKABOUT series.

Alex Kelly Ltd is based in Hampshire, in the south of England. They provide training and consultancy work to schools and organisations in social skills, self-esteem and relationship skills around the UK and abroad. They also provide speech and language therapy in a number of schools in and around the south west of England. Finally they run a day service for adults called Speaking Space which aims to support people with social and communication skills difficulties through group work.

Emily Dennis has worked in learning disability since 2008 in a variety of settings: residential, supported living, day services and special education. Within these she worked as a Communication Coordinator delivering training and implementing communication systems across Hampshire. This included projects around service user empowerment, enabling vulnerable adults to assertively make clear and informed choices about their lives. At university Emily studied BSc (Hons) Social Care Studies and specialised in learning disability and relationships. This led her to see the need for good quality, accessible sex education and

become passionate about creating a programme that would enable this. Emily worked for Alex Kelly Ltd from 2015-2018 as a project lead in sex and relationships. Their first book 'Talkabout Sex and Relationships 1' was published in 2017.

You can contact Alex through the website **www.alexkelly.biz**

Introduction to *TALKABOUT Sex and Relationships*: a word from Alex Kelly

The original TALKABOUT book was first published 20 years ago following a clinical study of social skills that I completed between 1991 and 1995. It was the first social skills package to give people a hierarchy to work through from self-awareness to assertiveness. Since then, my work in this field has developed and increased, and with this, so have the Talkabout products. Each Talkabout book is now aimed at a specific client group and has become more activity based with suggestions for games and activities for each topic. They are also more of a complete intervention package for teachers and therapists to use, including a scheme of work to follow throughout an academic year.

The other crucial development came in 2004 when I changed the hierarchy to include self-esteem and friendship skills. So the newer Talkabout books not only address self-awareness and social skills, but also self-esteem and friendship skills. And of course, I have always wanted to extend this to include intimate relationships but never felt I had the skill set to do this.

I then met Emily, who came to me with a proposal to increase the services we provide in our day service to include education in sex and relationships, and an idea was born! So for the past 3 years we have been busy... writing about sex and relationships, piloting our intervention and activities, and presenting to anyone who will listen to us on this subject. The result is too much to publish in 1 book, so we have divided it into 2 volumes: volume 1 is on relationships and this is volume 2 which is on sex education.

So this is the result of our work. We hope you like it but more importantly, we hope you find it useful.

Alex Kelly

Please feel free to contact me for more information or help with your work. My website is **www.alexkelly.biz**

The theory behind the book: a word from Emily Dennis

For many people with intellectual disabilities (learning disabilities), accessing accurate and unbiased sex education can be incredibly challenging. It is important to acknowledge how difficult and awkward it must be to ask a support worker or carer for information and advice on sex as it is an extremely personal and sensitive issue which many find embarrassing to discuss (Yacoub & Hall, 2009). Some people with learning disabilities therefore turn to their peers to ask questions about sex. Studies such as that by Yacoub & Hall have noted that there is often a great variation in knowledge and understanding of sex in people with learning disabilities. This may lead to these peers giving inaccurate, incorrect or contradictory information which could have dangerous consequences.

So what does history tell us about sex and people with a learning disability and how do we feel now, in today's society?

'Ordinary people leading ordinary lives' - this is the vision of people with learning disabilities in the 21st century. However, how do we really feel about adults with learning disabilities enjoying 'ordinary' sex lives?

Craft & Craft (1983) state that 'all humans have sexual drives' (Maslow, 1962, Wolfensberger, 1972). This is regardless of whether or not a person happens to have a learning disability. Craft & Craft (1982) also suggest that 'those who are mentally handicapped (sic) experience many of the same feelings and drives as the rest of the population, but commonly have been left in ignorance as to how to cope with them in a socially acceptable manner'. It could be argued that in many cases, this is still happening today.

In the 1980's Craft & Craft identified the 'Pandora's Box Complex' which suggests that there is a fear that people are unable to deal with the complexities of sex. In some cases sex was never mentioned in case it unleashed uncontrollable urges and sterilisation was often seen as a solution.

Thankfully attitudes in society have moved forward a great deal since then. However, it is still the case that although 'people with mild and moderate learning disabilities have the same rights, [...] they do not enjoy the same opportunities, to enter into sexual relationships as anyone else' (Brown & Benson, 1995).

Often professionals are not aware of the legislation and company policies (if available) surrounding the sexual relationships of the people they support. Murray et al (1999); cited in Grieve et al (2009) reported '47% of NHS staff and 16% of private sector staff were unsure or did not know their organisation's policies regarding client sexuality'. This study also found that 'a number of staff were also worried that that they could be disciplined, or even face prosecution if they condoned intimate relationships between people with learning disabilities in their care (2009). This is supported by Tindall (2015) who highlighted how 'safeguarding processes have created a climate of liability avoidance, with providers striving to reduce their exposure to criticism if something goes wrong'. The FPA's (2008) "It is My Right" campaign highlighted that a shocking 94 per cent of professionals think barriers exist that prevent people with learning disabilities from having relationships. 'Protecting people from all risks may seem like the safest thing in the short term, but can leave people more exposed to danger and abuse in the future' (Fanstone & Andrews, 2005).

Another consideration is sexual abuse and exploitation. As Fanstone & Andrews (2005) state: 'Sexual abuse and exploitation of people with learning disabilities is widespread and easy to cover up, leaving serious damage to people who are already 'vulnerable'. Firth and Rapley (1990) suggest that this makes it especially important to educate people with learning disabilities on their right to say no and methods of protecting themselves from this form of abuse. 'People with learning disabilities can be sexually exploited... the blame for this [is] largely [due to] the lack of sex education given to young people with learning disabilities' (McCarthy 1999, p.58). It is therefore of paramount importance that people with learning disabilities have the necessary skills, information and understanding to engage in sexual relationships without putting themselves, or others, in danger.

This means that sex education is a key component in keeping people safe but it is important to recognise that a single form of sex education may not be useful, accessible and understandable to everyone. There is no point in delivering sex education information which people cannot comprehend and is beyond their level of understanding (Cross, 1998). This is supported by the London School of Hygiene and Tropical Medicine (LSHTM) and University College London's recent study, claiming that sex education needs to become 'more graphic because teenagers are increasingly experimenting with taboo practices' often seen in pornography (The Telegraph, 2017). You cannot just educate people in the facts around sex without firstly equipping them in the skills necessary to enjoy an intimate relationship.

In March 2017 Sex education was made compulsory in all schools in England. The move follows months of campaigning, arguing that 'the current curriculum is years out of date and does not reflect the dangers faced by young people today' (The Independent, 2017). This will come into effect from September 2019. All children from the age of four will be taught about safe and healthy relationships and children in secondary schools will be given age-appropriate lessons about sex. This 'emphasises the central importance of healthy relationships' (www.gov.uk, 2017) before moving onto delivering interventions around sex education.

Confidence in delivering this type of work is also a big factor. This has been repeatedly highlighted by the problem of teacher embarrassment and lack of knowledge. Research with teachers in England has found knowledge levels seriously lacking. For example, in one study many teachers were confused about the difference between HIV and AIDS, with 6% failing to identify HIV as a sexually transmitted infection (Westwood and Mullan 2007). Teacher training does not necessarily include any content on SRE and only 3% of teachers reported that SRE was covered adequately in their Initial Teacher Training (Sex Education Forum, 2008).

For all these reasons, I feel passionately about the importance of sex and relationship education for people with learning disabilities and that this should be high quality, person-centred information available and accessible to all. So the 'Talkabout Sex and Relationships book 1 and 2' are the result of many years of work in this field and aims to support and equip group facilitators and parents to address this stigma and hopefully to gain confidence to provide proactive, rather than reactive, sex and relationship education. In this way, we can use the first book to develop their understanding of intimate relationships before moving on to developing their understanding of sexuality in this volume. In doing this, we will hopefully reduce the risk of abuse, and support people with learning disabilities to have happy, healthy relationships and lead truly 'ordinary' sex lives.

(👤) An overview of the book

TALKABOUT Sex and Relationships is the second of two books. The first covers 'Relationships' and this book covers 'Sex Education'. This is a practical resource that has been designed to help therapists and teaching staff to teach relationship skills in a more structured way, giving ideas on the process of intervention with lots of activities and worksheets to use at every stage. It is aimed at working with people in groups but can be adapted for working on a one-to-one basis.

Volume one is divided into 8 topics:

Assessment
Topic 1 Getting to know us
Topic 2 Staying safe
Topic 3 Introduction to relationships
Topic 4 Starting a relationship
Topic 5 Developing a relationship
Topic 6 Coping with problems
Topic 7 When a relationship ends
Topic 8 Looking to the future

Volume two is dived into 5 topics:

Assessment

This includes two assessments: a 1:1 interview and a friendship skills rating assessment. This provides you with a baseline score from which you can measure progress.

Topic 1 Working together

This level helps the group to get to know each other using activities that will focus on self-awareness, self-esteem and group gelling.

Topic 2 Personal identity

This level an understanding of oneself and one's own body, including activities around the life cycle, appropriate touch and staying healthy.

Topic 3 Let's talk about sex

This level aims to develop group members understanding of sex. From attraction and arousal to orgasm. Activities also cover masturbation and wet dreams.

Topic 4 Sex rules

This level improves awareness into the 'rules' around sex. Activities cover consent, public and private places as well as peer pressure and pornography.

Topic 5 Sex aware

This level improves understanding of sexual health including contraception, pregnancy and STIs.

Forms

In this section we have included formats for letters to parents / carers and session plans.

Who is *TALKABOUT Sex and Relationships* aimed at?

This resource is primarily aimed at young people or adults with a learning disability either in secondary education or adult services. We have piloted this resource with children in special schools (aged 13-18) and with adults (aged 18-35). However, we would extend this to include ages from 11 upwards depending on the individual.

When considering whether someone is suitable for this programme, it may help to ask the following questions:

- Do they struggle to make or keep friends?
- Are they isolated within their group?
- Do they struggle to understand appropriate relationships? E.g. what 'girlfriend/partner' means.
- Are they expressing interest in sex or intimate relationships?
- Are they exhibiting sexual behaviours?
- Are they vulnerable to sexual abuse?

The person should also have the following skills:

- Good self-awareness
- An ability to express themselves adequately in a group setting
- An ability to work within a group setting
- Motivation to attend a group

It is also important to remember that developing relationship skills should be seen within the context of the TALKABOUT hierarchy of intervention. This states that the pre-requisite skills of self-esteem and social skills should be taught prior to teaching sex and relationships.

The hierarchical approach to developing sex and relationships

Choosing the right place to start has to be the most important part of intervention as it is the difference between potentially setting someone up to fail or succeed.

Results from the social skills work in the early nineties led to the development of a hierarchy which is the basis of the 'Talkabout' resources. It was found that the success of intervention increased if nonverbal behaviours were taught prior to verbal behaviours, and assertiveness was taught last. For example, children working on their verbal or conversational skills progressed more if they already had good nonverbal skills, and children working on their assertiveness progressed significantly more if they had existing good nonverbal and verbal skills. In addition, it was found that a basic self and other awareness was important to teach as a pre-requisite to social skills training. A hierarchy was therefore proposed, piloted and found to be highly successful.

The hierarchy of social skills

Awareness of self and others

↓

Nonverbal behaviour or foundation skills i.e. body language and paralinguistic skills

↓

Verbal behaviour i.e. conversational skills

↓

Assertive behaviour

This is logical. Think about conversational skills; they are more complex than the nonverbal behaviours. For example, consider listening: a good listener uses appropriate eye contact and facial expression to show he is listening. Now consider turn taking: this needs good listening which in turns needs eye contact etc. So choosing the wrong skill to start work on, i.e. a skill that is too complex will potentially set a child up to fail.

A few years later, a link was noticed between children and adults with social skills difficulties and those with low self-esteem and friendship skills difficulties. These three areas are often very interlinked. Low self-esteem can result in poor social skills. Poor social skills can result in a lack of friends. A lack of friends can result in low self-esteem. So the hierarchy was updated to include all 3 aspects of work.

The hierarchy of social skills, self-esteem and friendship skills

Self-awareness and self-esteem

↓

Social skills (nonverbal, verbal and assertiveness)

↓

Friendship skills (friendship skills, intimate relationship skills and sex education)

Using this hierarchical approach, teachers or care workers are able to start work with the person at a level that is appropriate to their needs and progress up the levels to enable them to reach their full potential.

This does mean that if someone needs work on self-esteem or social skills, then you may need to refer to another Talkabout book before you work on sex and relationships. You may find it helpful to use the following questions to guide you with this:

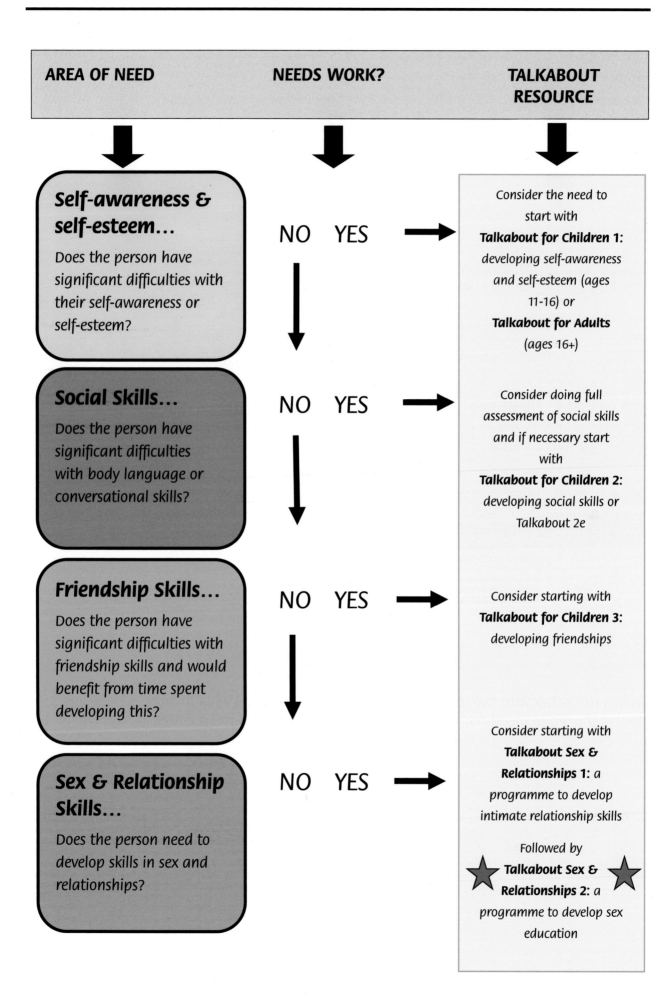

AREA OF NEED	NEEDS WORK?	TALKABOUT RESOURCE
Self-awareness & self-esteem... Does the person have significant difficulties with their self-awareness or self-esteem?	NO YES	Consider the need to start with **Talkabout for Children 1:** developing self-awareness and self-esteem (ages 11-16) or **Talkabout for Adults** (ages 16+)
Social Skills... Does the person have significant difficulties with body language or conversational skills?	NO YES	Consider doing full assessment of social skills and if necessary start with **Talkabout for Children 2:** developing social skills or Talkabout 2e
Friendship Skills... Does the person have significant difficulties with friendship skills and would benefit from time spent developing this?	NO YES	Consider starting with **Talkabout for Children 3:** developing friendships
Sex & Relationship Skills... Does the person need to develop skills in sex and relationships?	NO YES	Consider starting with **Talkabout Sex & Relationships 1:** a programme to develop intimate relationship skills. Followed by **Talkabout Sex & Relationships 2:** a programme to develop sex education

Setting up and running your relationships group

Here are a few guidelines for setting up and running your relationships group.

Group membership

It is important to match the group members in terms of their needs and also how well they are going to get on. A group is far more likely to gel and work well if they have similar needs, are a similar age and like each other. It is also important to consider gender of the group members and either have a single sex group or a group with a similar numbers of male / female members. Group membership should also be closed, i.e. you should not allow new members to join half way through as this will alter the group dynamics.

The size of the group

Groups work best if they are not too small or too big, preferably between 4 and 8. I usually aim for a group of 6. You need the group to be small enough to make sure that everyone contributes and feels part of the group and large enough to make activities such as role plays and group discussions feasible and interesting. Even numbers are helpful if you are going to ask them to sometimes work in pairs.

Length of the group

Timings are given at the beginning of each topic but it is important to remember that change will not happen quickly and you should allow time for group members to feel comfortable enough to talk about these issues. If you want to cover the entire content of this book, then you are probably looking at running the group for at least a year. In terms of the sessions, it is important that you have enough time to get through your session plan (see next section) but not so much time that the group members get bored. I usually aim for 45 minutes – 1 hour.

Group leaders

Groups run better with two leaders, especially as there is often a need to model behaviours, observe the group members, and facilitate group discussions. If you are able to have two group facilitators then ideally there would be one male and one female. This is not essential but can help with group discussions.

Accommodation

You will need a room that is comfortable for the group members to be in where you are not going to be interrupted. Don't be tempted to accept the corner of the hall or library as an acceptable place to run your group – this will not help your group members to relax and talk openly. In terms of the layout of chairs, I sometimes work around a table depending on the activity; however, it is usually helpful to start with the chairs in a circle for the group cohesion activity. I would also suggest that the group facilitators sit amongst the group members.

I always place a 'private' sign on the door to let people know that a session is in place (see activity 3) which can help the group members feel confident to speak out.

Cohesiveness

A group that does not gel will not learn or have fun. It is therefore important to take time to ensure that group gelling occurs. Things that help are:

- Interpersonal attraction – people who like each other are more likely to gel
- People who have similar needs
- Activities that encourage everyone to take part and have fun
- Arrange the chairs into a circle prior to the group
- Ensure that everyone feels valued in the group
- Ensure that everyone feels part of the group and has an equal 'say'
- Ask the group to set some rules
- Start each session with a simple activity that is fun and stress-free
- Finish each session with another activity that is fun and stress-free

The format of the session

The format of the session will vary from time to time but there are general guidelines which should be followed:

❶ Group cohesion activity

This is an essential part of the group. It brings the group together and helps them to focus on the other group members and the purpose of the group. The activity should be simple, stress-free and involve all.

❷ How are you feeling?

This should be done every session to ensure group members learn how to express their feelings and for the facilitator to address any concerns. Alternative feelings boards can be found in the TALKABOUT for Children and TALKABOUT for Adults books.

❸ Main activity(ies)

This will be your main focus of the session. It is during this part of the session that it is most important not to lose people's attention by allowing an activity to go on for too long, or one person to dominate the conversation.

❹ Finishing activity

Each session should end with a group activity to bring the group back together again and to reduce anxiety if the clients have found any of the activities difficult. The activity should therefore be fun, simple and stress free.

Abuse disclosure guidelines

Delivering work around sex and relationships may prompt disclosures of abuse. The group work provides a safe platform for this type of work and an environment to discuss negative experiences if they wish to.

 As you work through the resource you will notice the warning symbol in the instructions of activities which may prompt a disclosure. The idea is this will enable facilitators to prepare themselves so if they were to receive a disclosure they can react calmly and confidently.

Although facilitators should always be alert to the signs and signals of abuse, incidents may come to light during your sessions because a group member feels comfortable enough to disclose the information themselves. A disclosure can take place many years after the event or in an entirely different environment and it may be that the person now has the skills and confidence to share what has happened.

If someone discloses abuse to you

Do

- Remain calm.
- Listen carefully.
- Be aware that medical evidence may be needed.
- Reassure the person that they did the right thing to tell you, and that you will inform the appropriate person and the service will take steps to support and protect them.
- Write down what the person has told you as soon as possible.

Do not

- Promise to keep secrets; you need to pass this information on to the appropriate person.
- Ask any leading questions.
- Press the person for more information.
- Stop someone who is freely recalling information. They may not tell you the information again.
- Discuss the disclosure with anyone other than those you have a legitimate need to know.

At the first opportunity write down, sign and date the disclosure.

You should

- Write down exactly what the person has told you, using their exact words and phrases if possible.
- Note the setting and anyone else who was there at the time.
- Describe the circumstances in which the abuse came out.
- Ensure you separate factual information from your own opinions.
- Follow your own organisational policies and procedures.

Measuring outcomes

It is always important to be able to measure the success of any programme and this is no exception. With any of the Talkabout programmes, we encourage group facilitators to use pre and post assessment data to show progress. For this programme, you can use the Talkabout Assessment for Sex Education (pages 17–18) to show progress using the 6 point rating scale:

1. **Not present** – They are not able to demonstrate knowledge even with support / prompting

2. **Knowledge emerging** – They can give a basic answer with 1 or 2 ideas with prompting

3. **Knowledge developing** – They can give an adequate answer but it lacks detail

4. **Knowledge present in structured situation** – They can give a full answer within in a structured setting

5. **Knowledge present but not consistent** – They are not always able to use knowledge to act appropriately

6. **Knowledge present** – They are be able to show this knowledge and understanding in all settings

These scores can easily be transferred onto an excel spreadsheet to show data for either an individual or for groups.

If you would like support in setting up, running or evaluating any of your work in this area, we can support you. We regularly run courses throughout the UK, and sometimes abroad, on assessing and teaching social skills, and developing self-esteem and relationships skills. We can also support you to become a centre of excellence in this area by helping you to measure and evidence the effectiveness of your work. Please contact us through our website: **www.alexkelly.biz**

⊙ Assessment

Objectives   To provide a baseline assessment

Materials   1. 1:1 interview

                      2. Sex education rating scale

Timing   The timing of the assessment will depend on how well you
                      know the person. If you do not know them well, then you will
                      need to talk to a number of people and gain their opinions on
                      their strengths and needs.

ASSESSMENT

Activity	Description
1. 1:1 interview	Use the questions below to help find out whether the person has difficulties with intimate relationships and sexuality awareness. Make sure they feel relaxed and explain to them that you would like to ask them a few questions so that you can get to know them a bit better before you start working with them. You may choose to complete this interview after the first topic (working together) if you feel this would be more appropriate / easier.
2. Relationship skill assessment	This is a rating assessment of a person's understanding of sex and intimate relationships. It is a 6 point rating scale from 1: not present to 6: knowledge present. There are 3 sections: body awareness, sexual awareness and sexual safety. Some of the information will come from your 1:1 interview with the person but some will require you to talk to people who know the person well and your own observations. These ratings can then be transferred onto the Talkabout Assessment Summary wheel to provide you with a visual representation of their strengths and needs.
Author note	It is important to remember that some of these skills require pre-requisite skills which include self-awareness and social skills. If you consider the person to have significant needs in these areas please refer to the Talkabout books for developing self-awareness (Talkabout for Children 1 or Talkabout for Adults) and the Talkabout books for social skills (Talkabout 2e).

1:1 Interview

Name .... DoB ....

Completed by .... Date ....

INSTRUCTIONS: Sit somewhere nice and relaxing. Explain that you would like to ask them a few questions to get to know them better but that some of these questions are quite personal. This is because you are trying to find out who might be interested in developing their knowledge of intimate relationships. Reassure them that if they do not want to answer the question, then that is OK.

1 Tell me a bit about yourself. What do you like / not like? How old are you? Are you male or female? Child or adult?
2 Tell me about some of your relationships in your life. Who is really important to you? Who else is important in your life?
3 What do you think a 'good relationship' means?. Can you tell me what it might mean to you? What would you expect in a 'good relationship'?
4 Do you have a partner / boyfriend or girlfriend?? If not, would you like to have one? What would this mean to you? What would be good about having a partner?.

(continued)

5   Can you describe what the difference is between a friend and a partner?

What sorts of feelings do you have towards them? Are these the same of different?

6   What happens in an intimate relationship that doesn't happen with a friend?

What sorts of things do partners do together? How is this different to a friendship?

7   Can you tell me some ways in which we should try to keep safe in a relationship?

Think about going on a first date, keeping relationships happy and healthy, staying safe in a sexual relationship.

8   Sometimes things go wrong in a relationship, can you think of some things that might go wrong?

What about in a sexual relationship?

9   What could you do if things went wrong?

Who could you talk to? Where could you go?

10   Thank you for talking to me. Would you like to be part of a relationships group?

Is there anything you would like to know about relationships? What sorts of things do you think we should cover in the group?

BODY AWARENESS	1 Not present *They are not able to demonstrate knowledge even with support / prompting*	2 Knowledge emerging *They can give a basic answer with 1 or 2 ideas with prompting.*	3 Knowledge developing *They can give an adequate answer but it lacks detail*	4 Knowledge present in structured situation *They can give a full answer within a structured setting*	5 Knowledge present but not consistent *They are not always able to use knowledge to act appropriately*	6 Knowledge present *They are able to show this knowledge and understanding in all settings*
1. **SELF IDENTITY** *Can identify own age, gender, where they are in the life cycle*						
2. **BODY PARTS** *Can correctly identify the different parts of the body*						
3. **GENDER DIFFERENCES** *Is able to identify the difference between male and females bodies*						
4. **SEXUAL ORGANS** *Can identify and explain the functions of different sexual body parts*						
5. **BODY CHANGES** *Has an awareness of how bodies change i.e. puberty, pregnancy, menopause*						
6. **BEHAVIOUR AWARENESS** *Shows an understanding of appropriate touch with different people*						
7. **HEALTHY ROUTINE** *Shows an awareness of how to keep clean and healthy*						
8. **HEALTH SERVICES** *Shows an awareness of which services to access for different medical concerns*						

SEXUAL AWARENESS	1 Not present *They are not able to demonstrate knowledge even with support / prompting*	2 Knowledge emerging *They can give a basic answer with 1 or 2 ideas with prompting.*	3 Knowledge developing *They can give an adequate answer but it lacks detail*	4 Knowledge present in structured situation *They can give a full answer within a structured setting*	5 Knowledge present but not consistent *They are not always able to use knowledge to act appropriately*	6 Knowledge present *They are able to show this knowledge and understanding in all settings*
1. *FEELINGS OF ATTRACTION* shows an understanding of the difference between friendship and sexual attraction						
2. *SEXUALITY* shows an understanding of different types of relationship, e.g. heterosexual, homosexual, bisexual						
3. *AROUSAL* shows an understanding of what happens to body parts when aroused						
4. *SEXUAL ACTS* shows an awareness of different sexual acts						
5. *ORGASM* Shows an understanding of what happens to bodies when the height of sexual arousal is reached						
6. *MASTURBATION* Has an understanding of what masturbation is and where it would be appropriate						

SEXUAL SAFETY	1 Not present *They are not able to demonstrate knowledge even with support / prompting*	2 Knowledge emerging *They can give a basic answer with 1 or 2 ideas with prompting.*	3 Knowledge developing *They can give an adequate answer but it lacks detail*	4 Knowledge present in a structured situation *They can do only this spontaneously in a structured setting*	5 Knowledge present but not consistent *They are not always able to use knowledge to act appropriately*	6 Knowledge present *They are able to show this knowledge and understanding in all settings*
1. **AGE OF CONSENT** *Has an awareness of age of consent*						
2. **CONSENT** *Shows an awareness of consent through appropriate behaviours*						
3. **PUBLIC OR PRIVATE** *Can identify appropriate places for intimate acts*						
4. **PEER PRESSURE** *Able to recognize and handle different types of peer pressure appropriately*						
5. **INTERNET SAFETY** *Is able to recognize unsafe situations on the internet including pornography*						
6. **WARNING SIGNS** *Is able to recognize potentially unsafe behaviours in a relationship*						
7. **CONTRACEPTION** *Has an awareness of the function of contraception including protection against STIs*						
8. **PREGNANCY** *Shows an understanding of how babies are made*						

TALKABOUT Sex & Relationships Summary

Name .... DoB ....

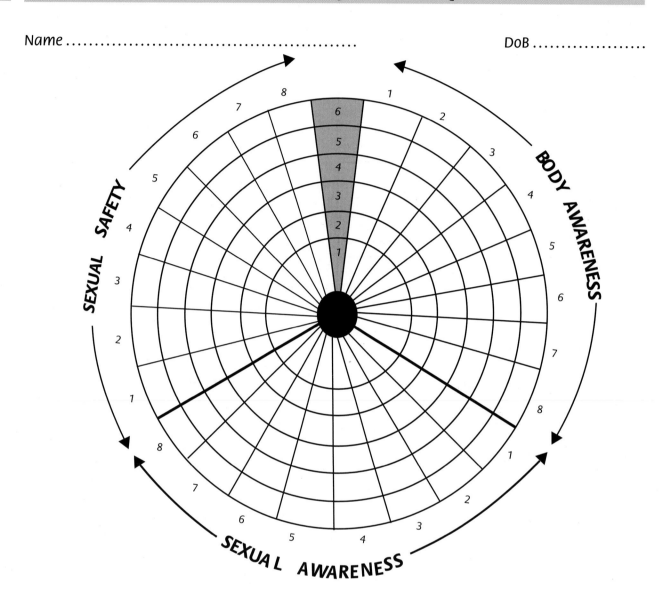

BODY AWARENESS	SEXUAL AWARENESS	SEXUAL SAFETY
1. Unsafe situations	1. Feelings of attraction	1. Age of consent
2. Strategies to stay safe	2. Sexuality	2. Consent
3. Talking to people	3. Arousal	3. Public / private
4. Internet behaviours	4. Sexual acts	4. Peer pressure
5. Information sharing	5. Orgasm	5. Internet safety
6. Consent	6. Masturbation	6. Warning signs
7. Behaviour awareness		7. Contraception
8. Body awareness		8. Pregnancy

Topic 1 Working Together

Introduction

The aim of this topic is to help the group to get to know each other using activities that will focus on self-awareness, self-esteem and group gelling. The main objective of this topic is for group members to start talking about themselves and to feel comfortable with each other. This topic also introduces the activity 'How am I feeling?' and the 'private' sign which you will then use at the beginning of every session.

Objectives
- To introduce awareness of self and others
- To gel the group
- To get to know a bit about each other
- To introduce the activity 'How am I feeling?'

Materials
- Print out and laminate activities as appropriate
- You will need Velcro™ to make up some of the activities
- Print out and photocopy worksheets as appropriate

Timing
- This topic will take up to 13 sessions to complete

Working Together

Activity	Description
How am I feeling? (Activity 1)	Pass the feelings board around the group and find out how everyone is feeling and why if they would like to share their reasons.
Pass it on (Activity 2)	The group hold hands in a circle and pass a squeeze around everyone and back to the person who started it.
The magic box (Activity 3)	The group pass an empty box around and group members take turns miming taking out an object that makes them happy. The group have to guess what the object is.
Throw the face (Activity 4)	A group member makes a facial expression and then mimes throwing that expression to another group member who then copies the facial expression. They then choose a new expression and pass that on.
High fives (Activity 5)	The group take it in turns to think of something great about another group member and pay them a compliment.
Detail detective (Activity 6)	The group are each given a topic. They then use their detail detective pad to find out everyone's favourite thing within that topic.
People around me (Activity 7)	Group members bring in photographs of people in their lives and arrange them onto their sheet in order of importance to them.
Trust top three (Activity 8)	The group use their sheets from the previous activity and choose the top three people they trust in their lives.
Trust is a-maze-ing (Activity 9)	Group members work in pairs to guide each other around a maze. They then discuss what qualities make someone trustworthy.

Activity	Description
Full of feelings (Activity 10)	The group expand their knowledge of different emotions by passing around a bag of cards, selecting one and sharing a time they have felt that emotion.
Group rules (Activity 11)	Group members discuss and agree what they think the rules should be for this group to maintain confidentiality and for everyone to feel safe and comfortable.
Private folder (Activity 12)	The group members make folders for their private work to be stored in.
Private group (Activity 13)	The group discuss how sessions should be private as you will be talking about sensitive issues. The group facilitator introduces the 'private' symbol and explains how it will be used each week.

Working Together

Activity 1: How am I feeling?

Preparation

Print out and laminate the feelings board. This board has five emotion choices and a question mark for 'other'. If you feel your group need a simpler or more complex board you could refer to Talkabout for Adults, Talkabout for Teenagers or Talkabout for Children Developing Self Awareness and Self Esteem for more choices.

Instructions

- Introduce the emotions and the facial expressions.

- Pass the board around the group members and ask them to say how they are feeling. Encourage them to ask each other.

- Can they share with the group why they are feeling that way?

- The '?' is for people to choose another emotion that is not on the board, for example they may be feeling 'hungry' or 'lonely'.

- This works well as a starter activity for each relationships session.

Activity 1: How am I feeling?

Sad

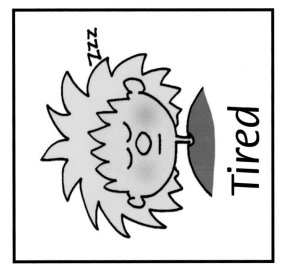

Tired

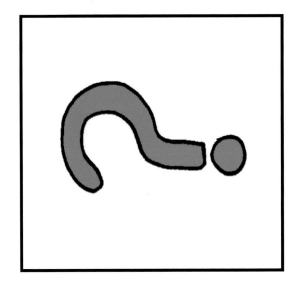

Worried

Happy

Angry

Activity 2: Pass it on

Preparation

This activity does not require any preparation.

Instructions

- The group should stand in a circle.

- Encourage group members to hold hands.

- Explain that you will be passing a squeeze around the group. When you feel the squeeze, pass it on to the person next to you.

- Continue until each group member has passed the squeeze.

- You could then go back the other way.

Variation

If any group members are uncomfortable with touch you could pass the Mexican wave instead. You could see how quickly you can go around the circle.

Activity 3: The magic box

Preparation

You will need an empty box for this activity. You may wish to decorate it with wrapping paper if you will be using it again.

Instructions

- The group should sit in a circle

- Introduce the magic box. Explain to the group that they will be acting taking something out of the box and the other group members guess what it is.

- The theme of today's session could be 'things that make us happy'.

- The facilitator should go first, by silently acting taking something out of the box which makes them feel happy.

- The group members should try to guess what it is.

- The box should then be passed on to the next person.

- Continue until each person has had a go.

Variation

You could repeat this activity with a variety of different themes, e.g. things that make us feel sad/angry/scared/excited, as well as favourite food, sports, animals, etc.

Working Together

Activity 4: Throw the face

Preparation

You will need a feelings board, a piece of flipchart paper and pens.

Instructions

- The group should sit in a circle with a table in the centre.

- Group members take it in turns to create a word shower of different emotions on a large piece of paper. You may wish to have a feelings board available to help generate ideas.

- The facilitator should start by saying a feeling and making the appropriate facial expression. It may be beneficial to start with something simple like happy or sad.

- The facilitator then acts pulling the expression from their face and throwing it towards a group member's face.

- The group member then acts catching the facial expression and putting it onto their own face. They then copy the facial expression that has been thrown to them.

- The group member now acts another feeling e.g 'grumpy' and makes the appropriate facial expression before acting peeling the expression from their face and throwing towards another group member.

- If group members are struggling to think of ideas, guide them towards the word shower of emotions the group made earlier in the session.

- Continue until each group member has had a go.

Activity 5: High fives

Preparation

This activity does not require any preparation.

Instructions

- The group should sit in a circle.

- Explain that you will be thinking about what is great about everyone in the group.

- The facilitator should ask the group to look around and choose a group member they would like to say something nice to. They should then ask if anyone would like to go first?

- The group member will then say 'yes, I would like to compliment X. I think X is great because … '.

- Continue around the circle until everyone has given a compliment. The group facilitator/s should go last and compliment anyone who may not have received a compliment yet.

- You could also guide the group by saying, 'Oh actually, X has already had a lovely compliment. Could I ask you to think of someone else in the group?'

Variation

Alternatively, you could do this as a finishing activity and say one thing that someone has done well in today's session.

Activity 6: Detail detective

Preparation

Print out the eight topic cards. You could enlarge them if this would help.

Instructions

- Explain to the group that they are going to be finding out more about each other today.

- Give each group member a topic card.

- Explain that they have to find out what each person's favourite thing is; e.g. if they have weather, they must find out what everyone's favourite weather is.

- The group can get up and move around the room to do this if they wish to.

- When everyone has completed their cards, the group can come back together and share what they have found. Are there similarities?

Extension activity

You may decide to print out a second set of the topic cards and repeat the activity finding out what everyone's worst things are.

Activity 6: Detail detective

Activity 6: Detail detective

Activity 7: People around me

Preparation

Each group member will need a worksheet enlarged to A3.

Group members should be encouraged to bring in photographs of their friends and family for this activity. You may need to photocopy and resize these prior to the session.

You will also need coloured pens or pencils, glue and scissors.

Instructions

- Introduce the session by telling the group that they will be thinking about different people in their lives and how important they are.

- Group members should then stick photographs or draw pictures of the different people in their lives in relation to how important they are.

- You may wish to start by thinking about family members, before moving on to friends, partners and professional relationships.

- Continue until each group member has completed their worksheet.

- Group members should then circle the people they trust the most.

- Group members can then share their worksheets with the rest of the group and discuss similarities and differences.

Activity 7: People around me

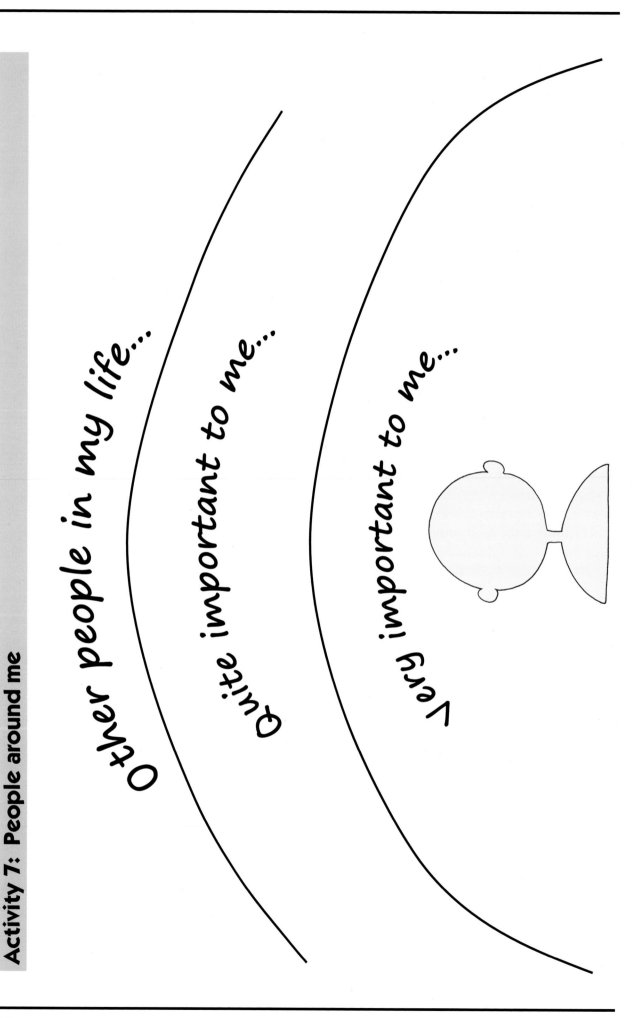

Other people in my life...

Quite important to me...

Very important to me...

Activity 8: Trust top three

Preparation

You will need a copy of the worksheet for each group member.

Also, the worksheets from Activity 7 'People around me' completed by everyone in the group.

Group members could bring in photographs of their family, friends and people that support them regularly.

Instructions

- The group should sit in a circle with a table in the centre.

- Explain to the group that today we will be thinking about our top three people that we trust in our lives.

- The group should revisit Activity 7 'People around me' from the previous session.

- Group members should now select the top three most trustworthy people in their lives, cutting out and sticking photographs onto the gold, silver and bronze boxes along with their names.

- Group members should then share their worksheets with the rest of the group and discuss.

Activity 8: Trust top three

Name: ....

Date: ....

Activity 9: Trust is a-maze-ing

Preparation

You will need to enlarge the 'Trust is a-maze-ing' worksheet to A3 size and print. You may wish to laminate this if you will be using it again.

You will need a counter to move around the board.

Instructions

- The group should sit in a circle with a table in the centre.

- Explain to the group that they will be doing an exercise around trust today.

- One group member should be blindfolded. Place their hand on the counter in the middle of the 'Trust is a-maze-ing' worksheet.

- Explain to the group member that they are in a maze and their fellow group members will help them to get out.

- The group members take it in turns to give the blindfolded person instructions to help them escape from the maze.

- Once they have successfully completed the maze, give that person a round of applause.

- Encourage them to say what they found helpful or unhelpful when the other group members were directing them. How did they feel being totally reliant on the other people in the group?

Variation

Alternatively the group could take it in turns to choose a fellow group member to look after a precious object for five minutes. Discuss why they chose that particular person and what qualities help us decide if someone is trustworthy. Continue until each group member has had a go.

Activity 9: Trust is a-maze-ing

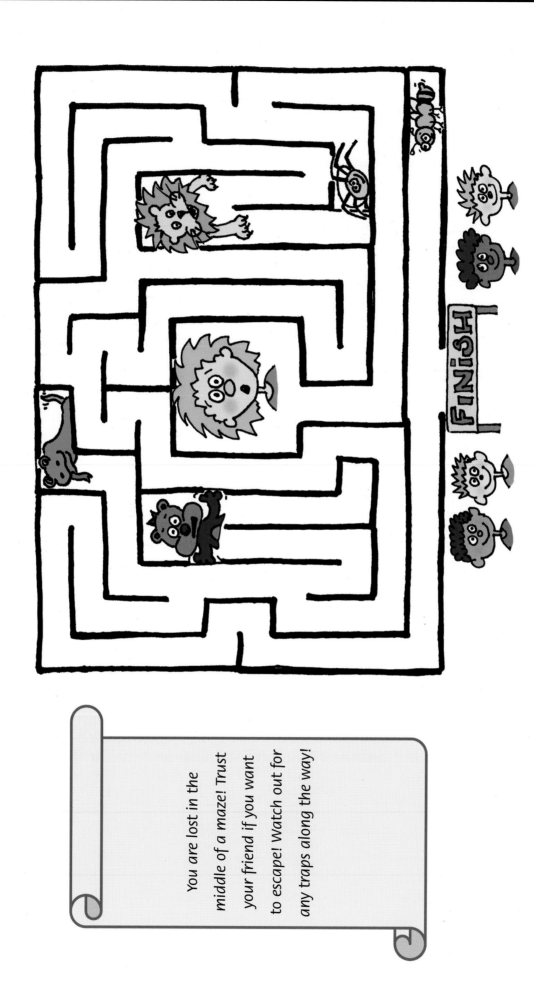

You are lost in the middle of a maze! Trust your friend if you want to escape! Watch out for any traps along the way!

Activity 10: Full of feelings

Preparation

Print out, laminate and cut out each emotion as a separate card.

You will also need a bag or hat to put all the cards in.

Instructions

- Introduce the session explaining that the group will be thinking about different types of emotions.

- Have the group sit in a circle and pass around the bag/hat containing all the emotions cards.

- The group take it in turns to select an emotion card and say if they have ever felt like that and if so, when. If the emotion is new to them you should discuss as a group what it means and other words you might use.

- Continue until everyone has had one or two turns each.

- Next lay all of the emotion cards out and as a group sort them into good/positive emotions and bad/negative emotions.

- Are there any other emotion words the group use? These could be added to the two piles.

Extension activity

As the emotions card page contains more words than on the feelings board (Activity 1) you may like to change and use this as your feelings board at the start of each group if the group members can cope with the additional choices.

Activity 10: Full of feelings

Excited 	Bored 	Out of sorts 	Fed up 
Hurt 	Loved 	Low 	Unwell 
Embarrassed 	Silly 	Good 	Rowdy 
Confused 	Irritated 	Nervous 	Crazy 
Sexy 	Frightened 	Proud 	Depressed 

Activity 11: Group rules

Preparation

Print out the worksheets so each group member has a copy.

Instructions

- It is important to establish some rules so group members know what is expected of them in the sessions.

- The group should be encouraged to come up with the rules themselves; however, group facilitators should guide them towards covering the following:

  1. *Confidentiality* – What we talk about in relationships group should stay within the group.

     (However, group facilitators may need to talk to other staff and pass on information if needed.)

  2. *Respect* – We should try to act and treat each other as adults.

  3. *Listening* – We should listen to one another and respect their ideas and opinions.

- Each group member should sign at the end to say they agree to try to keep to the group rules.

- The rules should be easily accessible in sessions; they could be on display on the wall, in group members' private folders or both. The group should also discuss what the consequence might be if someone breaks a rule.

Additional activity

If it would benefit the group you could complete a group contract. This can be especially useful if it is the first time the group has worked together.

You may also consider using a seating plan if you feel this will enable the group to be more productive.

Name: .... Date: ....

Relationship Group Rules

○

○

○

○

○

○

We agree to try to keep to the rules we have decided on as a group. Signed...

Date:..

© Alex Kelly and Emily Davies (2019) *TALKABOUT Sex & Relationships 2*, Routledge

Activity 11: Group rules

Name: .... Date: ....

Relationship Group Contract

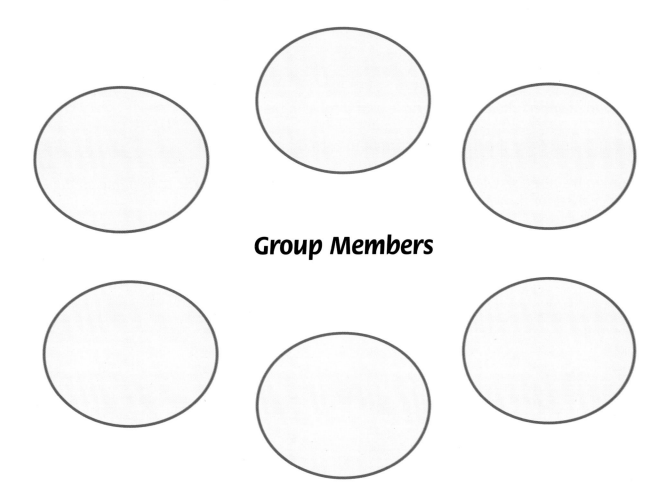

Group Members

We will meet every ....

from .... to ....

at..

Activity 12: Private folder

Preparation

You will need a folder for each group member.

Print out a 'private' cover sheet for each group member with a photograph for their individual folders.

Instructions

- Group members should sit in a circle with a table in the centre.

- Hand out a cover sheet and photograph to each group member.

- Group members should cut out and stick their photograph and write their name on the cover sheet for their folders.

- This will be a safe place to keep their work for the duration of the course.

Activity 12: Private folder

Relationships Group

Insert photo here

Name:

This is my private folder

Activity 13: Private group

Preparation

Print and laminate the private sign so it can be attached to the door of the room where the group is held each session.

Instructions

- Remind the group of the previous activity and that some topics they discuss in the group may be of a sensitive nature. Reassure the group and remind them that what is talked about in relationships group should be private.

  NB – group facilitators should then say that they may have to discuss what happens in the group with other staff if needed.

- Show everyone the private sign and explain that a group member should attach this to the door at the start and end of each session.

- This acts as a cue to the session beginning and ending as well as a reminder to others to knock before entering the room.

Activity 13: Private group

Relationships Group

Topic 2: Body awareness

Introduction

The aim of this topic is to introduce the group to the different body parts and to discuss and agree on the names and terminology they will then use for the rest of the course. The group look at how we keep ourselves safe in terms of touch and physical contact with others and also how we keep ourselves healthy. The topic then ends by looking at the human life cycle and how our body changes over time.

Objectives
- To introduce body parts and vocabulary
- To agree terminology to use in the group
- To understand how our bodies change over time
- To know how to keep our bodies safe and healthy

Materials
- Print out and laminate activities as appropriate
- You will need Velcro™ to make up some of the activities
- Print out and photocopy worksheets as appropriate

Timing
- This topic will take up to 17 sessions to complete

Activity	Description
It's a boy/girl thing (Activity 14)	Group members think about the differences between males and females and then sort the group into these two categories.
Puzzle parts (Activity 15)	The group select puzzle pieces of a male or female body and must work together to put the images back together again.
Body bits (Activity 16)	Using the images of a male and female, the group label a number of body parts including basic and more personal areas. The group then discuss different terminology for these parts and decide on the words they will now use in sessions.
Body Bingo (Activity 17)	Each group member is given a board containing a number of different body parts. The group then play a game of bingo with the person who covers up all the squares on their board first the winner.
Every-body's different (Activity 18)	The group complete a quiz around body image, voting true or false for each statement.
Touch talk (Activity 19)	The group begin thinking about 'ok' and 'not ok' touch, shading in a body map where different people can touch them and where they can't.
Ok touch (Activity 20)	The group choose three people from their 'People around me' sheet and decide what types of touch would be ok with each of them.
Caressing couples (Activity 21)	The group now consider a partner and think about what touches would be ok with them and what they should remember.
Healthy me! (Activity 22)	The group discuss what 'healthy' means and then using an outline of a body, think about different body parts and how we keep them healthy.
My routine (Activity 23)	Using a worksheet, the group consider what they do to stay healthy on a daily, weekly, monthly and 'sometimes' basis and who may need to help.

Body awareness

Activity	Description
How do they help? (Activity 24)	Thinking about their daily routine the group pick one aspect and consider who could help them and how if they needed support.
Lumps and bumps (Activity 25)	The group cut out images to create an information story about keeping our private body parts healthy and checking for signs something might be wrong.
Valued visits (Activity 26)	The group sort a number of scenario cards into the most appropriate place you might need to visit e.g. the doctor, hospital, sexual health clinic.
Helpful health (Activity 27)	Thinking about the places you could visit described in the previous activity, the group compile a list of all their local services including addresses and telephone numbers.
Life cycle (Activity 28)	The group sort a number of picture cards to show the human life cycle discussing each stage as they go.
Story of my life (Activity 29)	Group members create a book showing the life cycle and all the different stages including pictures of themselves for each stage if possible. The group then consider each stage and what you could do at that age.
Champion of change (Activity 30)	The group consider the two life stages of puberty and menopause and what happens at each stage to males and to females.

Activity 14: It's a boy / girl thing

Preparation

Enlarge the worksheet to A3.

You will need to print and cut out a picture of each group member.

Instructions

- Introduce the session by telling the group that they will be thinking about whether we identify ourselves as male or female.

- The group should sit in a circle.

- The group facilitator should place the worksheet in the centre of the group and talk through the differences between males and females. How do we know who is who?

- Group members should be given their picture and asked to place it on the worksheet showing whether they are male or female.

- Group members should then, if appropriate, explain why.

Author note

We need to be mindful that some people may not identify themselves as the gender they were born into. Depending on your knowledge of the people in your group and their ability, you may wish to have a discussion around this.

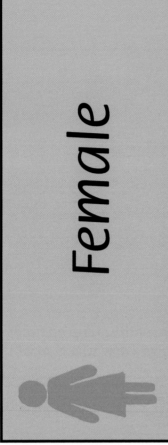

Female

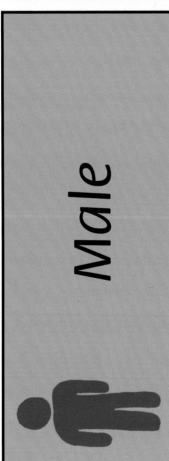

Male

Activity 15: Puzzle parts

Preparation

You will need to print out the pictures and laminate them. Cut them into pieces to create a puzzle. You can make the pieces as small or as complicated as you wish according to the group.

You may wish to find a hat or bag to place the puzzle pieces in.

Instructions

- The group should sit in a circle with a table in the middle.

- The group then pass around a bag or hat with the puzzle pieces inside. You may wish to do this to music and when the music stops a group member takes a piece.

- The group member should look at the piece and decide whether they think this is the front or back of a person and whether it is a male or female.

- Discuss this as a group.

- Continue to take puzzle pieces until four puzzles have been made: male and female front and back.

- The group should discuss the differences between the male and female bodies.

Variation

If the group are finding the activity particularly easy you may wish to cut the puzzle pieces even smaller to make it more challenging.

Activity 15: Puzzle parts

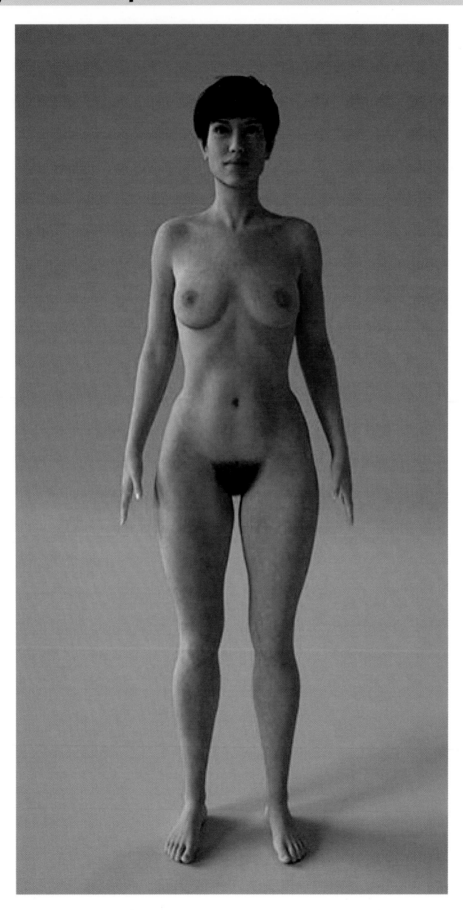

Activity 15: Puzzle parts

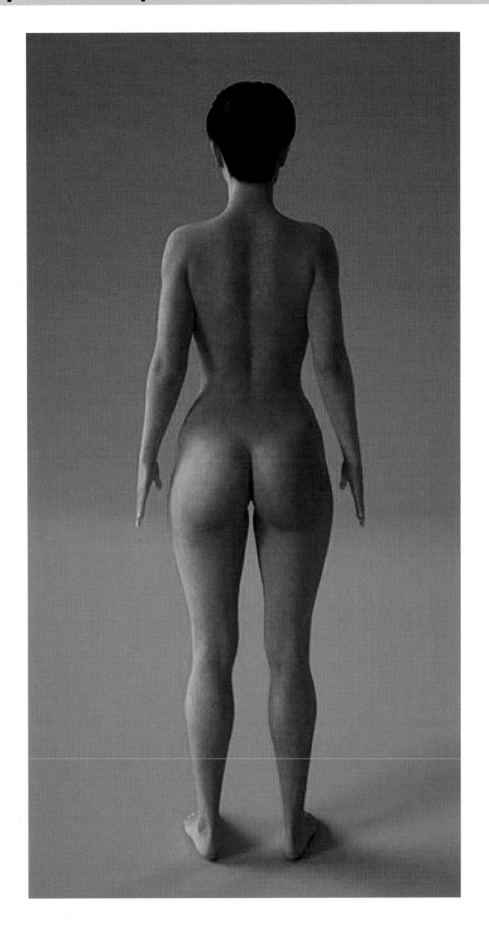

Activity 15: Puzzle parts

Activity 15: Puzzle parts

Activity 15: Puzzle parts

Body awareness

Activity 16: Body bits

Preparation

Enlarge a male and female worksheet to A3.

If you will be using these again you may want to laminate them and use a dry wipe pen.

Instructions

- Introduce the session by telling the group that you will be thinking about body parts today.

- The group should sit in a circle with a table in the centre.

- The group facilitator should place one of the worksheets in the centre of the group.

- Group members take it in turns to write on the worksheet, labelling the different body parts.

- The group can add extra labels if they wish.

- Once each body part has been labelled ask the group to list other names that we may use for that body part.

- You may wish to start with less explicit body parts such as tummy / stomach / belly.

- Reassure the group that in this session they are allowed to say rude names that they have heard for explicit body parts.

- Once each of the worksheets is competed for different body parts, the facilitator should read through the different words group members have come up with. It is OK to have a bit of a giggle at this stage.

- Group members should now tick or underline the terminology they prefer and discuss why. It is also an opportunity to discuss why we wouldn't use some words as they can be rude or offensive.

- The group should now decide on one word they all agree on for each personal body part. Explain that actually the medically correct term is often best so then everyone knows exactly what we mean.

- This will be the terminology the group will use for the duration of the course.

Activity 16: Body bits

Name: .... Date: ....

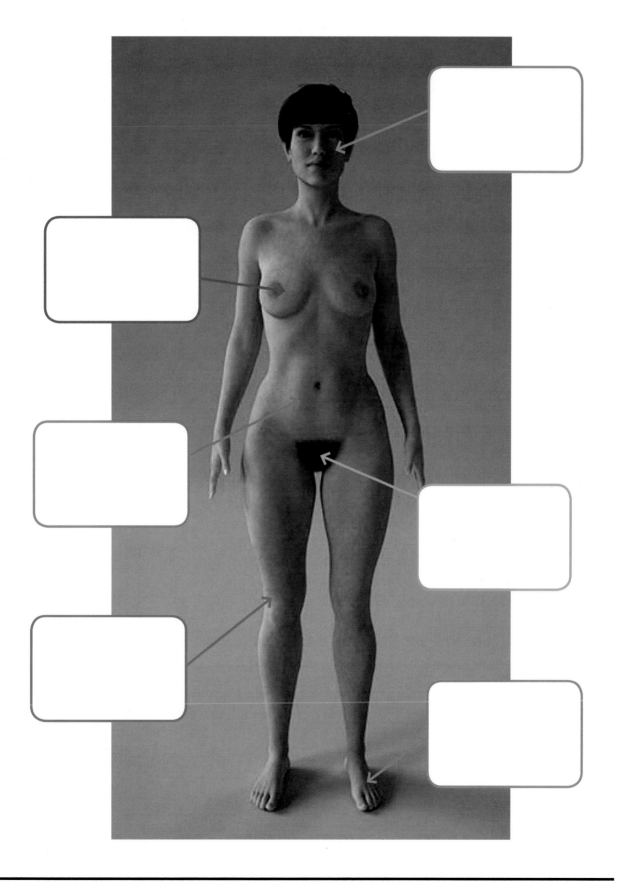

Activity 16: Body bits

Name: .... Date: ....

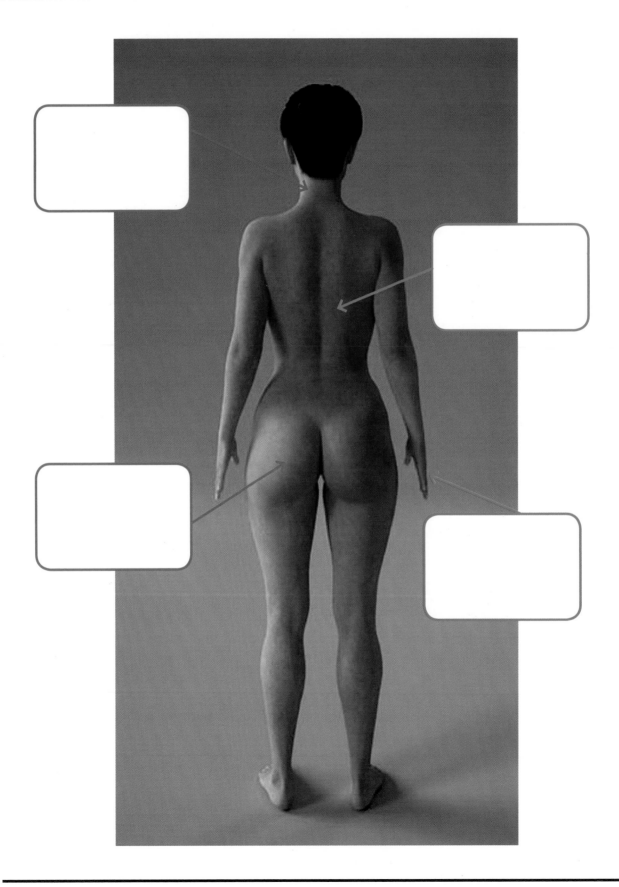

Activity 16: Body bits

Name: .... Date: ....

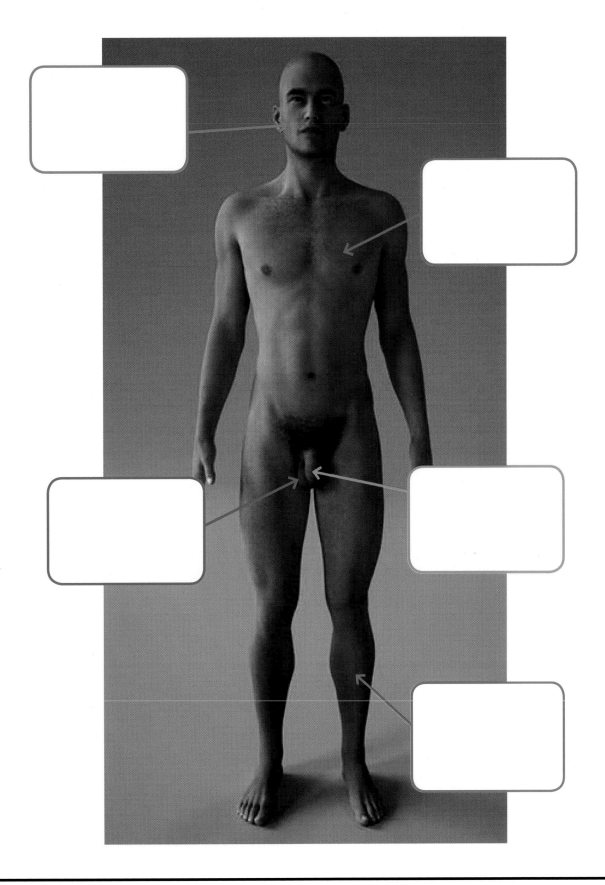

Activity 16: Body bits

Name: .... Date: ....

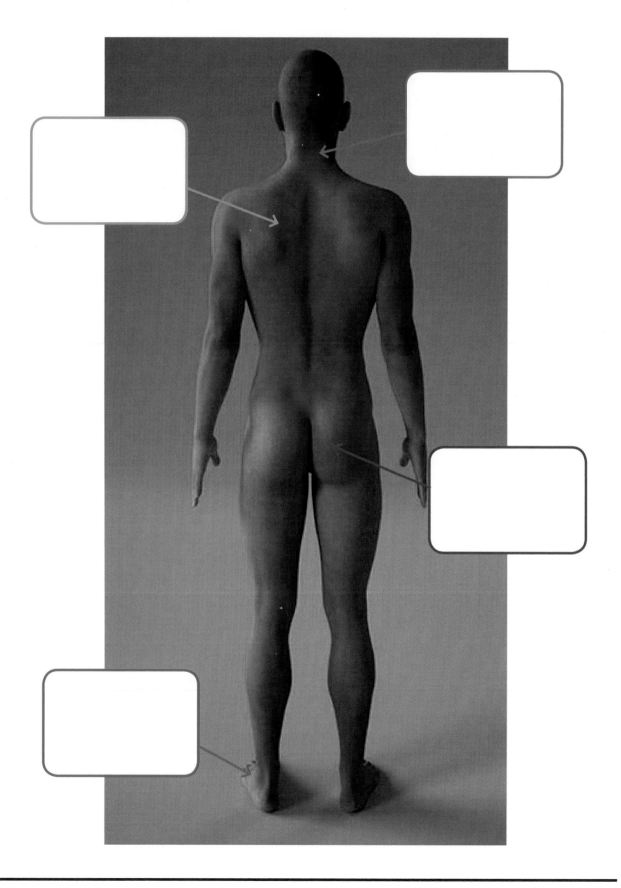

Activity 17: Body bingo

Preparation

Print and laminate the bingo sheets. You may need two of each sheet depending on group size.

Print, cut and laminate one of each body part. You will need a hat or bag to place these in.

You will need counters or buttons, or you should cut out squares of paper for group members to cover the body parts with when they have been called out.

Instructions

- Introduce the session by telling the group that you will be thinking about body parts today.

- The group should sit in a circle with a table in the centre.

- The group facilitator should pass around the bag of body part cards with each group member taking one out and saying the name for that body part.

- Once the different body parts have been introduced, the group member should hand out the bingo sheets, one per person.

- The counters should be placed in the centre.

- The group member will now pick a card from the bag and show the group. Each person who has this body part on their bingo sheet should take a counter and cover the correct picture on their bingo sheet.

- Continue until one group member has counters over all the body parts on their bingo sheet. This group member can now call out 'bingo'.

- It is recommended that rather than finish the game here, you continue to call out the body item cards until every group member has completed their sheet and can call out 'bingo'

NB

You may get a bit of giggling and silliness around some of the private body parts. Reassure the group that this is OK but it is important that we get to know the names for the different parts of the body.

Activity 17: Body bingo

Activity 17: Body bingo

Activity 17: Body bingo

Activity 17: Body bingo

Activity 18: Every-body's different

Preparation

Print out and laminate the 'true' and 'false' cards so there are enough for group members to have one of each. You could attach them to lollipop sticks so group members can hold them up to vote if they think a statement is 'true' or 'false'.

Instructions

- The facilitator should explain to the group that today they will be looking at body image.

- Hand out a 'true' or 'false' voting stick to each group member. You may wish to do a few practice runs such as 'It is Monday today' or 'My name is Bob', etc.

- Read through the questions and ask group members to vote, indicating whether they think the statement is true or false.

- Discuss each statement as a group before reading out the answers.

- Finish with a light-hearted game or activity. Group members could go around the room saying one nice thing about themselves.

Activity 18: Every-body's different

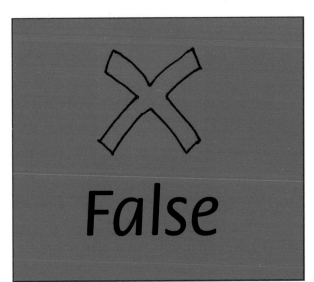

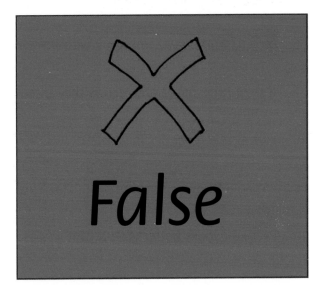

Activity 18: Every-body's different

Quiz

1. The average dress size for a woman is size 10.

2. The average shoe size for a man is size 9.

3. Shop mannequins represent the body of an average woman.

4. The average height for a man is 6 ft 2.

5. The average woman's bust size is 34B.

6. 50% of women are unhappy with how they look.

7. If men have big feet it means they also have a big penis.

8. Slim is always sexier in women.

9. 75% of images in fashion magazines are airbrushed.

10. Everyone looks better with a tan.

Activity 18: Every-body's different

Answers

1. False! The average woman's dress size is size 16; in 1957 it was a size 12.

2. True! However, in 1967 the average shoe size was size 7 for men.

3. False, research by the University of Liverpool found that the average female mannequin used to model clothes in UK clothes stores is the size of a 'severely underweight' woman. In some high street stores the mannequin's waists are only 23.5 inches – the approximate measurements for a 7-year-old child!

4. False, the average height for a man in 2017 is 5 ft 10.

5. False, this was the case in 1957 but the average bust size is now 36DD.

6. False! Approximately 91% of women are unhappy with their bodies and resort to dieting.

7. False! A study by University College London found there was no correlation between foot and penis size.

8. False! In many countries such as Fiji, Jamaica and Afghanistan plus-size woman are far more attractive. It is said to show wealth, good health and fertility.

9. False! Actually 100% of images in fashion magazines have been retouched. Studies show that 70% of women report feeling depressed after reading these magazines.

10. False! In Western cultures many people feel having a tan is desirable. However, in Asian cultures paler skin is more attractive as it means you are wealthier and can stay indoors; tanned skin would show you are from a poorer class as you would be working out in the fields.

Body awareness

Activity 19: Touch talk

Preparation

Enlarge the worksheet to A3.

You will need to print several copies or laminate it to reuse.

You will need red, orange and green felt tips or dry wipe pens if you are using a laminated copy.

You will need a tissue box which will be used as a dice. Place a square of hook Velcro™ on each face of the dice.

Print, laminate and Velcro™ the people cards with loop Velcro™.

Instructions

- Introduce the session by telling the group that they will be thinking about who can touch us where on our bodies.

- The group should sit in a circle.

- The group facilitator should place one of the worksheets in the centre of the group and talk through the different body parts.

- A selection of people cards should be attached to the tissue box dice.

- Group members take it in turns to roll the dice.

- They should then colour the worksheet green where they think it is OK for that person to touch and red where it would not be OK for them to touch. You may also choose to use orange to show where it might sometimes be OK to touch. For example, group members may shade personal body parts in orange for the doctor to touch; this would be OK if you had a problem, or needed a test for this body part but not OK if you were to go in with an eye condition.

- Discuss differences in opinion with the group; however, some touches would never be OK with certain people.

- The facilitator should then swap over the people cards and pass the dice to a different group member to roll.

Activity 19: Touch talk

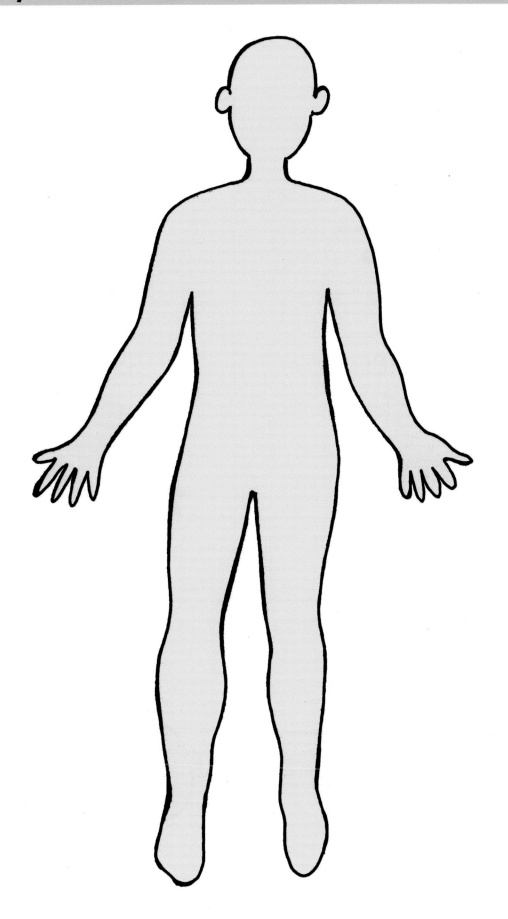

Activity 19: Touch talk

Mum

Dad

Brother

Sister

Best Friend

Partner

Activity 19: Touch talk

Grandma

Grandad

Male Support Worker

Female Support Worker

Social Worker

Advocate

Your dreams and wishes are...

Activity 19: Touch talk

Housemate

Neighbour

Taxi Driver

Teacher / Tutor

Niece / Nephew

Celebrity

Activity 19: Touch talk

✂

Doctor	Nurse

Dentist	A stranger

Partner who you live with	Husband / Wife

Activity 20: OK touch

Preparation

Each group member will need a copy of the worksheet and their individual completed copy of Activity 7 'People around me'.

If possible, group members should bring in pictures of the people on their 'People around me' sheet to use in this activity.

Instructions

- Group members should choose three people from their 'People around me' sheet.

- Encourage group members to choose a person from each section: 'Very important to me', 'Quite important to me' and 'Other people in my life'.

- They should then stick photographs of these three people onto the worksheet or write their names if they don't have pictures.

- Group members should then think about what touches or interactions would be OK and add three ideas for each person. Ideas could include:

  - Secret handshake
  - Kiss
  - Hold hands
  - High five
  - Touch private parts
  - Have sex
  - Say hello

  - Link arms
  - Stroke hair
  - Tickle
  - Hug
  - Kiss cheek
  - Stroke arm

- The group should then compare and discuss the activity.

Activity 20: OK touch

Name: .... Date: ....

I could...

_____

_____

I could...

_____

_____

Me

I could...

_____

_____

A Stranger

I could...

_____

_____

Activity 21: Caressing couples

Preparation

You will need a copy of the worksheet for each group member.

Group members should be encouraged to bring in a picture of a partner if applicable.

You may need the ideas sheet of different touches / interactions from the previous activity.

Instructions

- In this activity the group should consider which touches would be OK with a partner.

- The group should be encouraged to bring in a photograph of a partner, if applicable.

- If group members do not have partner at the moment they can draw their perfect partner in the box on the worksheet.

- The group should then think about four touches they feel would be OK with a partner and add these to the boxes around the partner. They could choose to write these or draw a picture.

- Group members should then complete the 'What should I remember?' box at the bottom of the worksheet. Ideally the group would come up with something along the lines of asking a partner if they would like to do one of the touches, listening to them and respecting their wishes. This starts to introduce the topic of consent.

Activity 21: Caressing Couples

Name ....

Date ....

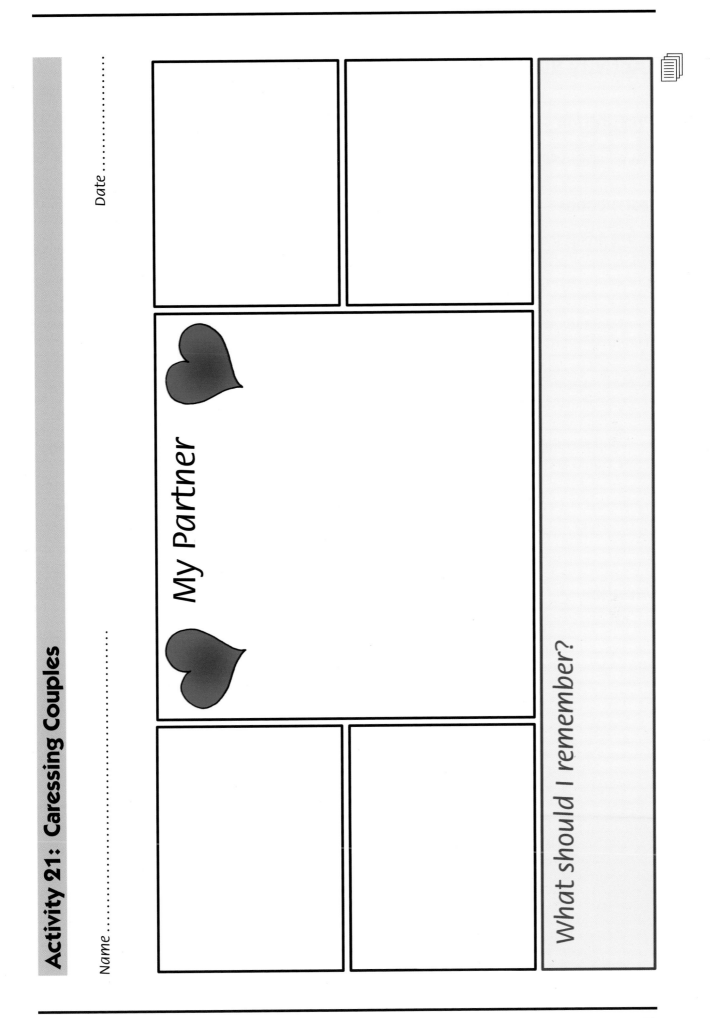

My Partner

What should I remember?

Activity 22: Healthy me!

Preparation

You will need pens and several pieces of flipchart paper.

Instructions

- The group should sit in a circle.

- Explain that today they will be thinking about what 'healthy' means.

- As a group, write down ideas around the following questions: 'What is a healthy person?' and 'What do we do to stay healthy?' Write these on pieces of flipchart paper.

- Next, tape a couple of sheets of flipchart paper together and either draw a silhouette of a body or draw around a group member.

- Group members should then take it in turns to choose a part of the body and write on how we would keep that part healthy, e.g. 'hair – wash regularly'.

- This activity could be either simplified or made more complex depending on the ability of the group.

Variation

You may wish to have one female and one male body silhouette. Group members should discuss the similarities and differences. For example, both sexes would need to clean their teeth but women would use sanitary products to keep clean and healthy while on their period.

Activity 23: My routine

Preparation

Enlarge the 'My routine' worksheet to A3 and print out a copy for each group member.

You will also need to print out the ideas sheets for each group member.

Instructions

- The group should sit in a circle.

- Explain that today we will be looking at things we do to stay healthy on a daily, weekly, monthly and 'sometimes' basis.

- Group members should either write ideas onto their worksheets or cut out and stick cards from the ideas sheets onto the appropriate section.

- There are blank cards for group members to write or draw any additional ideas.

- Once everyone has completed their worksheet, ask people to feed back their ideas. Discuss similarities and differences.

- Now start a discussion about which of these things we might need help with. We all have our own strengths and weaknesses; something one of us finds easy might be difficult for someone else and vice versa.

- Consider how this might change if we were to become unwell or break our arm. Which things might change and why?

Activity 23: My routine

Name ....

Date ....

Daily	Weekly	Monthly	Sometimes

Activity 23: My routine

Shower 	Bath 	Wash face 
Wash hair 	Brush teeth 	Change underwear 
Cut nails 	Hair cut 	Dental check up 
Doctor's appointment 	Eye test 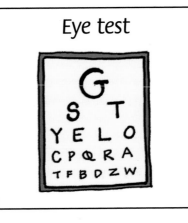	Take medication 

Activity 23: My routine

| Do exercise | Hair removal | Eat fruit and veg |
| Brush hair | Change clothes | Drink water |

Activity 24: How do they help?

Preparation

You will need to print out a copy of the worksheet for each group member.

Alternatively you may wish to laminate the worksheet and use dry wipe pens if this will be a group activity.

Instructions

- Ask the group to think back to Activity 23 'My routine', considering which aspects of their day they need support with. If this is not applicable, ask group members to think about if they had broken their leg, what would they need support with?

- Group members should think about one activity they might need support with, e.g. showering, and write this into the 'What?' section.

- They should now think about who they would like to support them with this; there might be several options, for example 'mum or a female member of staff'. They should then write this under the 'Who?' section.

- Next, group members consider how they would like to be supported and write this under the 'How?' section. For example, shutting the door, handing me the flannel, shutting the shower curtain, giving me instructions of where I should be washing.

- Finally, discuss what you should do if anything other than this happens. Depending on the ability of the group you may discuss how something like forgetting to pass you the conditioner might be OK as you could ask for it but touching your private areas in a sexual way would never be OK. You should say no and tell someone you trust.

- You may wish to repeat this exercise with different scenarios.

Activity 24: How do they help?

Name .... Date ....

What?

Who?

How?

 If something different happens say no and tell someone you trust!

Activity 25: Lumps and bumps

Preparation

You will need to print a copy of the cards and worksheets for each group member. You will also need scissors and glue.

If you are doing this as a group activity you should enlarge the cards and worksheets to A3. You may wish to laminate and put Velcro™ on the back of the cards and in the boxes if you will be using this again.

Instructions

- The group should sit in a circle with a table in the centre.

- Explain to the group that they will be looking at staying healthy in more detail today and focusing on our private parts.

- Group members should cut out the different cards and match them up to the statement on the worksheet, getting them into the correct order.

- Group members should then feed back their worksheets. You may wish to discuss certain stages in more detail.

- There are lots of great easy-read resources online which can support the group to find out more.

Activity 25: Lumps and bumps

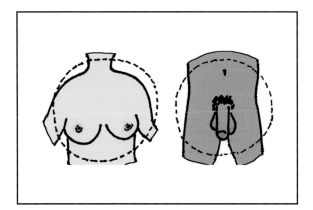

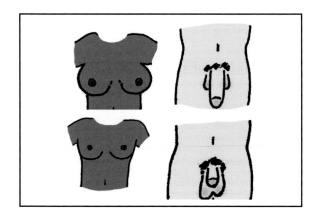

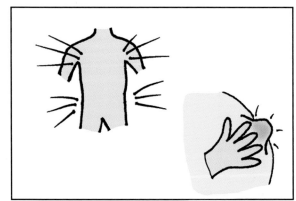

Activity 25: Lumps and bumps

Name . . . .   Date . . . .

1. Everyone is different, this makes us all unique!

2. You should get to know your body.

3. You need to check for differences like a lump, pain, swelling or skin changes.

4. Check the surrounding areas too.

Activity 25: Lumps and bumps

Name .... Date ....

5. You should check your body once a month.

6. Check in a private place like your bedroom or when you are in the shower or bath.

7. If you notice something different, tell someone you trust.

8. Go to see your doctor.

Activity 26: Valued visits

Preparation

You will need a copy of the places and scenario cards. You may wish to laminate these if you will be using them more than once.

You will also need a copy of the worksheet for each group member.

Instructions

*   Group members should sit in a circle with a table in the centre.

*   Read through the eight place cards and lay them out on the table.

*   Place the scenario cards face down, in a pile on the table.

*   Group members take it in turns to pick up a scenario card and read it aloud. They should then consider where they might go if they were in that situation. You may find there is more than one appropriate place for some situations; for example, if you have had unprotected sex you could go to a pharmacy, walk-in centre or sexual health clinic.

*   Continue until all the scenario cards have been used.

*   Group members should now pick a scenario and complete a worksheet, thinking about where they might go and what might happen. Group members may need to look online to research what might happen in some scenarios. (Remember to only use reputable websites.)

Body awareness

Activity 26: Valued visits

Author note – reputable websites

There are billions of different websites on the internet. Anybody can set up a website and publish anything they want. Information on the internet isn't always true, so look out for the signs of an accurate website.

The most reliable websites are often set up by official organisations and businesses. They can often be identified by their web address.

Suffix	Example
.com	The 'standard' ending to a web address often used by commercial organisations
.org	Generally used by not for profit organisations
.co.uk	A company's website based in the UK
.gov	A government organisation, e.g. local council
.ac.uk or .sch.uk	University, schools and colleges

Also remember:

- Check the date – make sure you aren't getting out-of-date information; look for a 'last updated' date on the page or site.

- Does it look professional? - If a site looks poorly designed and amateurish, chances are it was created by amateurs. It is best to avoid it and look for something better.

- Does it sound professional? – is it well written or are there lots of spelling and grammatical mistakes? Again, try to avoid websites like this.

Activity 26: Valued visits

 Doctor

 **Hospital**

 **Pharmacy**

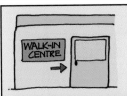 **Walk-in centre**

 **Sexual health clinic**

 Dentist

 First aider

 Other

Activity 26: Valued visits

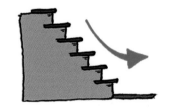

You think you might have an STI.	You have a bad cold.	You think you / your partner might be pregnant.
You think you have broken your toe.	You have found a lump in a private area.	You have had a bad headache every day for the last 2 weeks.
You have back pain.	You have fallen down a flight of stairs.	You have been in a car accident.
You get bitten by a dog.	You get stung by a bee.	You get sunburn.

Activity 26: Valued visits

You have a bad headache. 	You have cut your finger while cooking. 	You have had unprotected sex. 
You have tooth ache. 	You have hit your head and feel sick. 	You have a sore throat. 
You have broken your arm. 	You have an itchy rash all over your body. 	You have an upset stomach. 
You have a splinter in your finger. 	Your tooth has fallen out. 	You have a swollen eye. 

Activity 26: Valued visits

Name . . . .   Date . . . .

> **What's wrong?**

↓

> **Where should I go?**

↓

What might happen?

Activity 27: Helpful health

Preparation

You will need to print a copy of the worksheet for each group member.

Instructions

- Group members should sit in a circle with a table in the centre.

- Re-cap on the previous activity, thinking about which health services we would go to in different situations.

- Group members should complete a worksheet looking at their local health services. Some they might already know, such as their doctor's surgery, dentist and hospital, but some they may need to research online.

- Group members should write the name and address of each local health service onto the worksheet. It may also be useful to include phone numbers and websites.

- The worksheets can then be kept in group members' private folders for reference.

Activity 27: Helpful health

Name . . . .   Date . . . .

My local doctor's surgery is...

My local hospital is...

My local pharmacy is...

My local walk-in centre is...

My local sexual health clinic is...

My local dentist is...

Activity 28: Life cycle

Preparation

Print and cut out the Life cycle cards. You may wish to print in card and laminate if you will use these again.

You will need a piece of string / washing line and pegs.

Instructions

- The group should sit in a circle with the table in the centre.

- Lay the Life cycle cards face down on the table.

- Group members take it in turns to take a card and decide where they feel that stage comes in the life cycle.

- Discuss any differences in opinion within the group.

- Group members should then peg the Life cycle cards onto the washing line once they have all agreed on the correct order.

- Discuss each stage as a group.

Activity 28: Life cycle

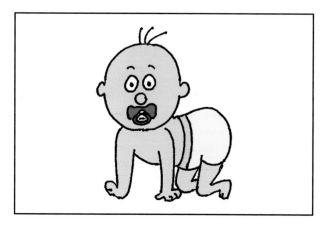

Activity 29: Story of my life

Preparation

Group members should bring in photographs of themselves at different stages of their lives.

You will need to print out a workbook for each group member.

You may also wish to print, cut out and laminate a picture of each life stage (baby, child, teenager, etc.)

You will need scissors, pens and glue.

Instructions

- Introduce the session by telling the group that you will be thinking about how we change throughout our lives.

- Lay out the life stages cards randomly and ask the group to place them in the correct order.

- You may wish to pin these to a washing line or length of string, to act as a prompt once sorted correctly.

- The group should then work through the different life stages considering what they could do at that age (i.e. babies can cry, crawl). These could be written out on a spare piece of paper if necessary.

- Group members should then cut and stick photographs of themselves at that life stage and write what age they were.

- If group members have not yet reached certain life stages (e.g. adult or older person) they could draw a picture of how they imagine they may look at that age.

Activity 29: Story of my life

Activity 29: Story of my life

Insert photo here

This is me!

I am .... old

Stage One - Baby

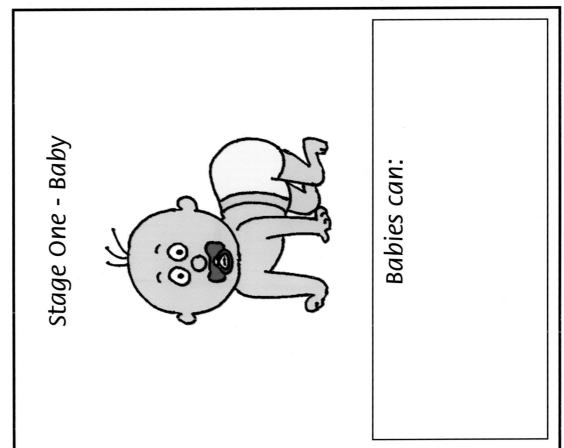

Babies can:

Activity 29: Story of my life

Insert photo here

This is me!

I am .... year old

Stage Two – Child

Children can:

Activity 29: Story of my life

Insert photo here

This is me!

I am / will be .... years old

Stage Three - Teenager

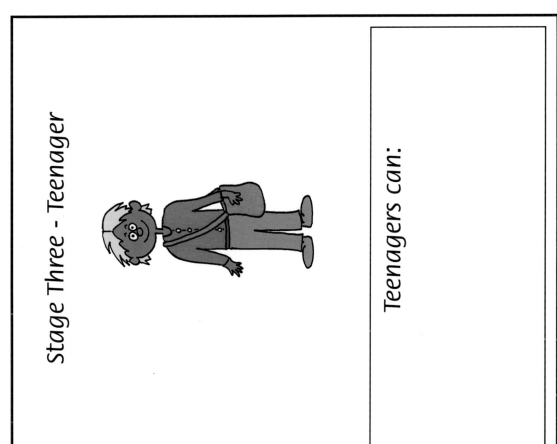

Teenagers can:

Activity 29: Story of my life

Stage Four - Adult

Stage Four - Adult

Insert photo here

This is me!

I am / will be .... years old

Activity 29: Story of my life

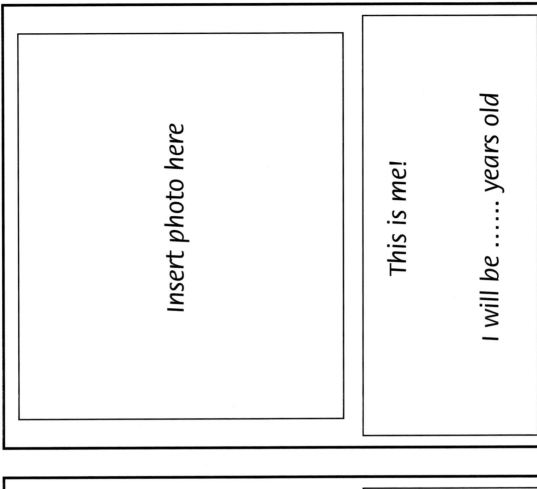

Insert photo here

This is me!

I will be .... years old

Stage Five – Older Person

Older people can:

Activity 30: Champion of change

Preparation

You will need to enlarge and print the 'Champion of change' worksheet and ideas sheet to A3 size for each group member.

You may wish to laminate and Velcro™ these if you will be using this as a group activity or using it again.

You will also need scissors and glue.

You may wish to have flipchart paper and pens to write down ideas.

Instructions

- The group should sit in a circle with a table in the centre.

- Explain to the group that they will be doing an exercise around changes today.

- The group should write a list of ideas that they associate with 'puberty' and then 'menopause', including what it is and whom it affects.

- Group members should then complete their worksheets by sorting ideas and sticking onto either the 'puberty' or 'menopause' section.

- There are also blank cards for group members to add any of their own ideas.

- When everyone has finished, the facilitator should then call out the different words or phrases from the ideas sheet. Group members can vote as to whether they feel this is something that might happen either in puberty or menopause.

Activity 30: Champion of change

Name ....

Date ....

Menopause

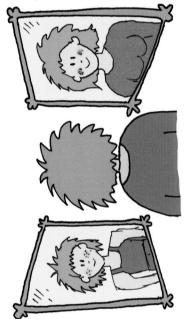

Puberty

Body awareness

Activity 30: Champion of change

Changing from a child to an adult	A change in a woman's life where periods stop
	Periods start (women only)
Hair grows under arms and on private parts. Hair also grows on faces for men	Penis / breasts grow
	Greasy hair
	Mood swings
	Spots
Unable to have a baby	May have difficulty sleeping
	Hot flushes
Voice breaks (men only)	
	Private parts become dry or sore

Topic 3: Let's talk about sex

Introduction

The aim of this topic is to help the group understand what sex is including all parts from attraction to arousal, intercourse and orgasm. The group talk about what happens and why as well as the different sexual acts that might occur as well as intercourse. The group then also consider what masturbation is and what is appropriate as well as what is meant by a 'wet dream'.

Objectives
- To consider the difference between friend attraction and sexual attraction
- To know what happens to our bodies when we are aroused
- To understand what sex is
- To understand what masturbation is and what is appropriate

Materials
- Print out and laminate activities as appropriate
- You will need Velcro™ to make up some of the activities
- Print out and photocopy worksheets as appropriate

Timing
- This topic will take up to 10 sessions to complete

Let's talk about sex

Activity	Description
Annabelle's attraction (Activity 31)	The group read a story about Annabelle's attraction to Kian and Felix and discuss how this differs and what it means.
Friend or fancy (Activity 32)	Group members discuss the difference between attraction to a friend and sexual attraction and create a definition for both. They then discuss what qualities they find attractive in others.
Recognising relationships (Activity 33)	The group consider different types of relationships such as straight, gay, bisexual and define these visually using the worksheet.
Terms of arousal (Activity 34)	Using a set of cards, the group consider what arousal means and then sort 'slang terms', 'old fashioned terms' and 'correct terms'.
Aroused anatomy (Activity 35)	The group begin by agreeing an appropriate definition for arousal and then split into two teams to discuss and label what happens to a female body when it is aroused and a male body.
What is sex? (Activity 36)	The group play a snap activity matching images to their definitions to introduce what sex is and also sexual acts such as oral sex and anal sex.
Sex terms (Activity 37)	Using a set of cards, the group consider different words people say to mean sex and then sort them into 'slang terms', 'old fashioned terms' and 'correct terms'.
The big O (Activity 38)	The group begin by discussing what they think 'orgasm' means and then order a set of cards to describe an orgasm and what happens.
Masturbation musts (Activity 39)	The group begin by deciding on an appropriate definition for masturbation and then sort cards into what is and isn't masturbating. They can then consider when and where this is appropriate.
Wet dreams (Activity 40)	The group reads a story about William's wet dream and consider what happens and why.

Activity 31: Annabelle's attraction

Preparation

You will need to print a copy of the story. You may wish to laminate this if you will be using it again.

You will need to print a copy of the worksheet for each group member or enlarge it to A3 for a whole group activity.

Instructions

- Group members should sit in a circle with a table in the centre.

- The facilitator should read the story of Annabelle's attraction aloud to the group.

- Group members should consider Annabelle's attraction to both Kian and Felix and add ideas mentioned in the story onto the worksheet.

- Group members should feed back their ideas and discuss any differences in opinion. Is Annabelle attracted to both in the same way or are they different?

Activity 31: Annabelle's attraction

Annabelle

Annabelle works at her local café. She loves her job and also enjoys spending time with her colleagues as they all get on well. She gets on particularly well with Kian and Felix.

Kian is really kind to her, helping out whenever he can and making her laugh. They often meet up after work and watch their friend's band as they both love music. They have known each other for years and used to go to school together. Annabelle is always happy when spending time with Kian.

Felix has been working at the café for a couple of years. Annabelle loves chatting to him about cycling as they are both members of the local cycling group. Last week they completed a charity bike ride together and raised lots of money. Felix is also very handsome; he has dark brown eyes, thick brown hair and a lovely toned body from all this cycling. He also has a beautiful smile. Every time Annabelle sees him she gets a fluttery feeling in her stomach.

Activity 31: Annabelle's attraction

Name: ....

Date: ....

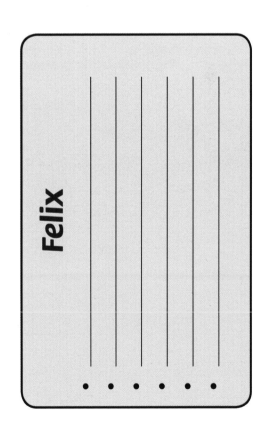

Kian

Felix

Activity 32: Friend or francy?

Preparation

You will need to print a copy of the worksheet for each group member.

Instructions

- Group members should sit in a circle with a table in the centre.

- The group should think back to the story of Annabelle's attraction and consider how she felt about Kian and Felix. Discuss whether she was attracted to them both in the same way, or in different ways.

- Group members should complete a worksheet for both friendship attraction and sexual attraction and decide on a definition for both. Ideas you could discuss may include:

■ Makes you laugh	■ Trustworthy	■ A good body
■ Kind	■ Honest	■ Lovely smile
■ Similar interests	■ Confident	■ Smells nice
■ Thoughtful	■ Fun to be with	■ Good dress sense
■ Friendly	■ Nice hair	■ The right height
■ Easy to talk to	■ Beautiful eyes	■ The right age

- Discuss other things group members find attractive, such as muscular physique, tattoos, facial hair, etc.

- Group members should feed back their ideas and discuss any differences in opinion.

Activity 32: Friend or fancy?

Name: ....

Date: ....

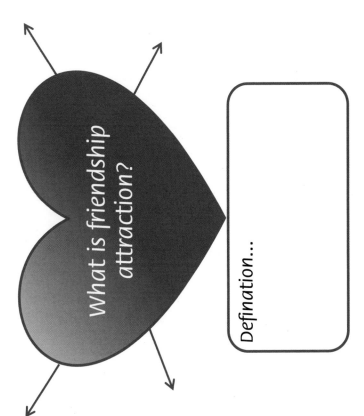

What is friendship attraction?

Defination...

Activity 32: Friend or fancy?

Name: ....

Date: ....

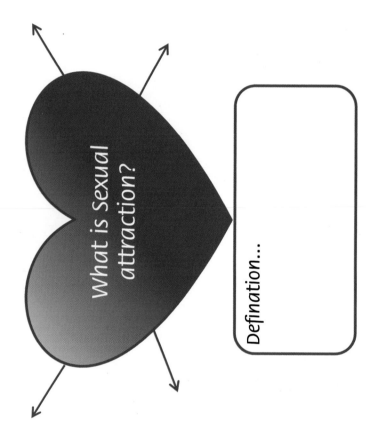

What is Sexual attraction?

Defination...

Activity 33: Recognising relationships

Preparation

You will need to print, laminate and cut out the 'recognising relationships' symbols.

You will need to print a copy of the worksheet for each group member.

Instructions

- The group should sit in a circle with a table in the centre.

- Explain to the group that today they will be thinking about whom we are attracted to in more detail and the different types of relationship.

- The facilitator should introduce the concepts of 'heterosexual', 'gay', 'lesbian' and 'bisexual' relationships using the different symbols.

- Using the relationship symbols, group members work in pairs to create different relationships. The facilitator should ask each pair in turn to show a 'heterosexual', 'gay', 'lesbian' or 'bisexual' relationship.

- The rest of the group should then say if they agree or help them to get the correct answer.

- Reinforce the message that all these different relationships are normal and 'OK'.

- Group members could then complete a worksheet, matching up the different types of relationship. These can then go into their private folders.

Activity 33: Recognising relationships

Activity 33: Recognising relationships

Name: .... Date: ....

Match up the different types of relationship!

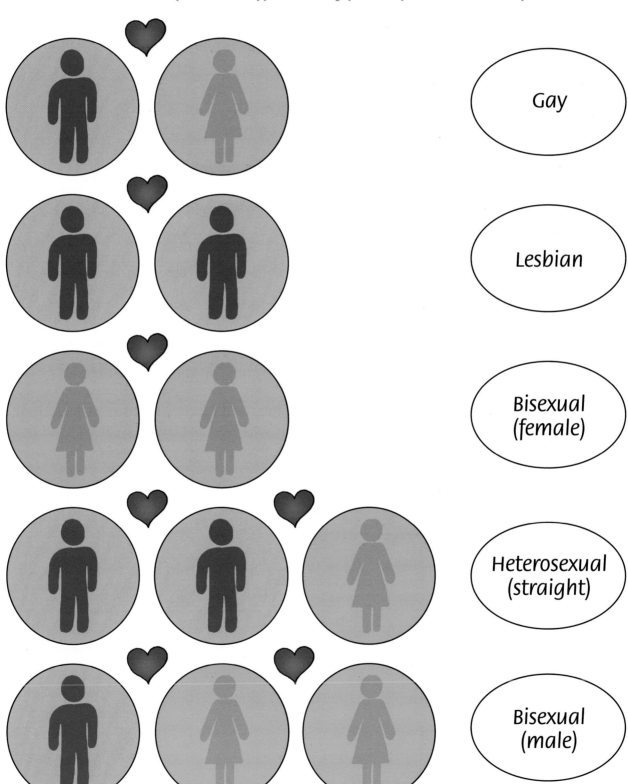

Activity 34: Terms of arousal

Preparation

Print and cut out the terms of arousal and category cards. You may wish to laminate these if you want to use them again.

You may also like to use a piece of flipchart paper and pens to write down ideas.

Instructions

- The group should sit in a circle with a table in the centre.

- Explain to the group that they will be doing an exercise around arousal today.

- Group members consider what the word 'arousal' means, adding ideas to a piece of flipchart paper.

- The facilitator should then introduce the three categories: 'Correct terms', 'Old-fashioned' and 'Slang', explaining what they mean.

- The group members then take it in turns to pick a 'Terms of arousal' card, read it aloud and decide which category it fits into.

- You may wish to add any additional ideas the group came up with and sort these.

- Discuss with the group why it is important to use the correct terms; this way we know that we won't upset people by using offensive language and everyone will be clear on what is being discussed

Activity 34: Terms of arousal

✂

Horny

Steamy

Randy

Sexy

Frisky

Turned on

Hot

Racy

Erotic

Aroused

Hot to trot

Lusty

Activity 34: Terms of arousal

✂

Raunchy

Correct terms

Old-fashioned

Slang

Activity 35: Aroused anatomy

Preparation

You will need a sheet of flipchart paper and some marker pens.

You will also need to enlarge to A3 and print two copies of the worksheet, one for a male and one for a female body.

Instructions

- Group members should sit in a circle with a table in the centre.

- The facilitator should recap on attraction and explain that this session will explore what happens to our bodies when we are attracted to someone. Reassure the group that although this is a subject many of us find embarrassing or funny it's really important that we understand the changes to our bodies and why this happens.

- Group members should work together to come up with words they associate with arousal and write them onto the sheet of flipchart paper. The group should then decide on a definition.

- The group should now discuss what happens to our bodies when we become aroused. Is this the same for both males and females?

- Split the group into two teams. You may wish to have one female and one male team or mixed depending on the dynamics and make up of your group. It is OK for the teams to have a bit of a giggle and a laugh so long as they can still focus on completing the work.

- Give each team a worksheet and tell them if they have a male or female body. The teams should then label their worksheets with the different body parts that change when aroused, what happens and why. Groups then look up more information either in books or online; however, ensure you give the groups a list of reputable websites beforehand.

- When both teams have finished, rejoin as a whole group with each team feeding back their worksheets.

- Finish with a fun and light-hearted game or activity.

Activity 35: Aroused anatomy

Name: ....   Date: ....

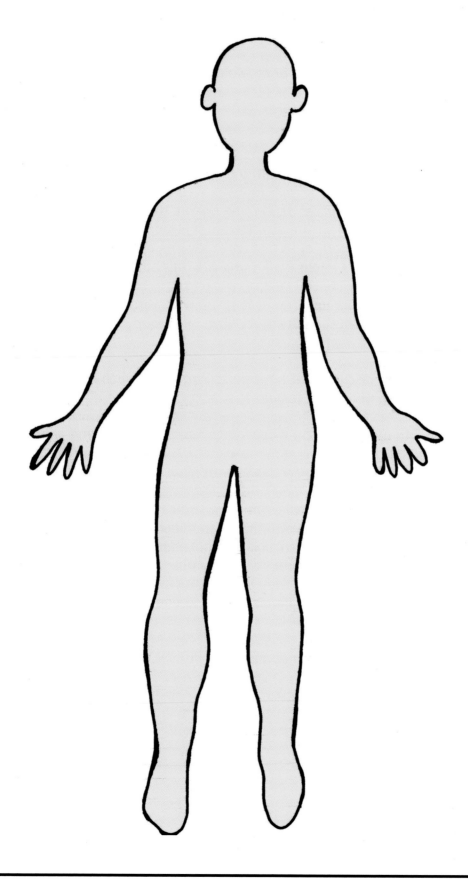

Activity 36: What is sex?

Preparation

You will need a piece of flipchart paper, pens, scissors and glue.

Print and cut out the 'What is sex?' cards. You will also need a set of the large body parts cards.

Print a copy of the worksheet for each group member as well as two copies each of the smaller body parts sheet each.

Instructions

- The group should sit around a table for this activity.

- Explain to the group that they will be exploring 'What is sex?' today.

- As a group, consider the reasons why people might have sex and add these ideas to a piece of flipchart paper. Ideas might include that it feels nice, to feel close to their partner, to try to make a baby, etc. It is important to discuss that for many couples sex is an enjoyable activity and without the purpose of conceiving a baby.

- Place the 'What is sex?' cards face down on the table. Play a 'snap'-style activity taking it in turns to match the pictures and definitions. Continue until all the cards and their definitions have been paired up.

- Each time a pair is created, talk through the definition and discuss it as a group making sure everyone understands.

- Next, place the large body part cards on the table. Ask each group member in turn to use the body parts to create a different sexual act, e.g. sexual intercourse, oral sex, anal sex, touching.

- Group members then complete their own worksheets using the smaller body part images to create examples of the different sexual acts.

- These worksheets can now go into group members' private folders.

Variation

Print two copies of the large body part cards and attach them to two tissue boxes. Use these as two dice taking it in turns to roll them and see if they match, e.g. penis and bottom is anal sex.

Activity 36: What is sex?

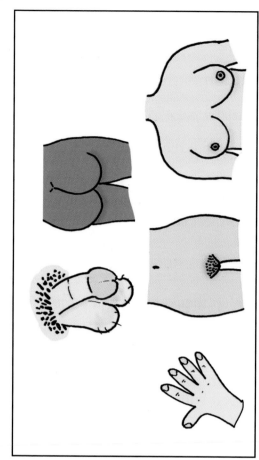

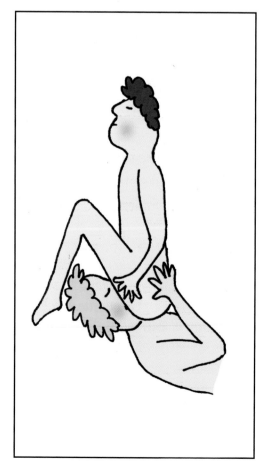

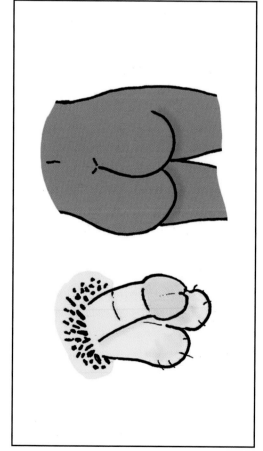

Activity 36: What is sex?

Oral sex

When a man's penis or a woman's vagina is pleasured by someone's mouth.

Vaginal sex

When a man and a woman have sex the penis goes inside the vagina.

Anal sex

When a man's penis goes inside someone's bottom.

Touching

When someone's vagina, penis, breasts or bottom is pleasured by someone's hand.

Activity 36: What is sex?

✂

Penis	Vagina
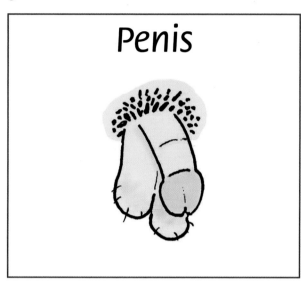	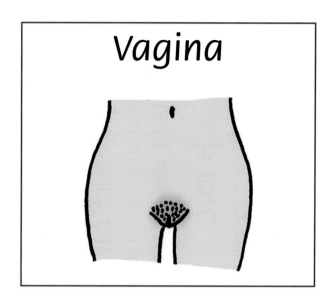
Breasts	Bottom
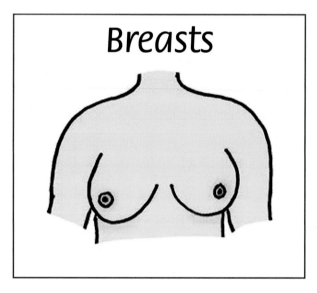	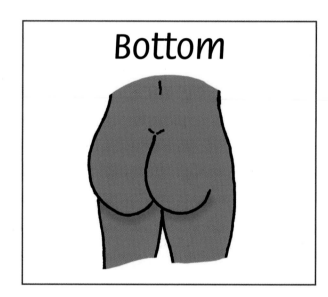
Hand	Mouth
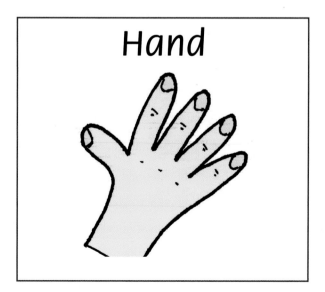	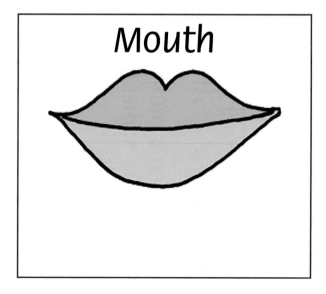

Activity 36: What is sex?

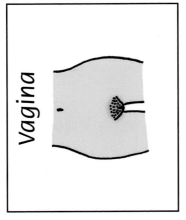

Vagina

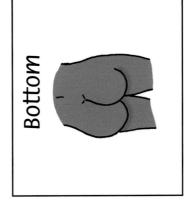

Bottom

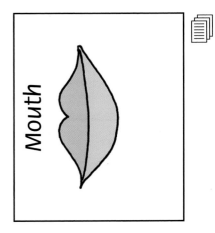

Mouth

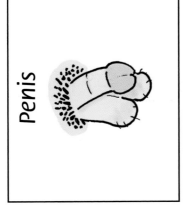

Penis

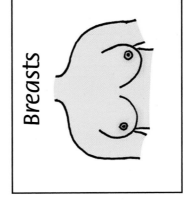

Breasts

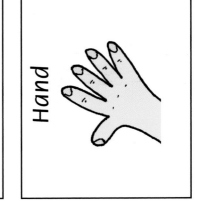

Hand

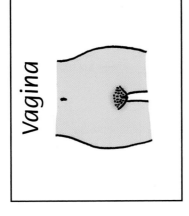

Vagina

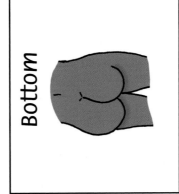

Bottom

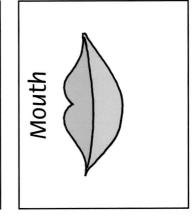

Mouth

Penis

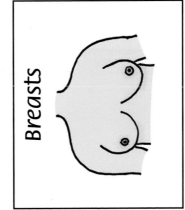

Breasts

Hand

Activity 36: What is sex?

Name: ....   Date: ....

	+	**= Vaginal sex**
	+	**= Anal sex**
	+	**= Oral sex**
	+	**= Touching**

Activity 37: Sex terms

Preparation

You will need to print and cut out the 'sex terms'. You may wish to laminate these if you will be using them more than once. You will also need the category cards from Activity 34.

You may also like to use a piece of flipchart paper and pens to write down ideas.

Instructions

- The group should sit in a circle with a table in the centre.

- Group members consider what the word 'sex' means, adding ideas to a piece of flipchart paper.

- The facilitator should then re-introduce the three categories 'Correct terms', 'Old-fashioned' and 'Slang' from Activity 34, explaining what they mean.

- The group members then take it in turns to pick a 'sex terms' card, read it aloud and decide which category it fits into.

- You may wish to add additional ideas the group came up with and sort these too.

- Discuss with the group why it is important to use the correct terms. This way we know that we won't upset people by using offensive language and everyone will be clear about what we are discussing.

Activity 37: Sex terms

✂

Make love

Sleep with

Get laid

Bang

Boink

Tap

Hump

Shag

Get some

Do it

Get it on

Go all the way

Get in their pants

Activity 37: Sex terms

Screw

Sexual intercourse

Coitus

Sex

Nail

Dip the wick

How's your father

Hanky panky

Knock boots

Score

Hook up

Fool around

Fornication

Activity 37: Sex terms

✂

Nookie

Copulation

Shaking of the sheets

Doing the dirty

Baby making

Special cuddle

Consummation

Bone

Activity 38: The big O

Preparation

You will need a sheet of flipchart paper and some board pens.

You will need to print, laminate and cut out the cards.

Instructions

- The group should sit in a circle with a table in the centre.

- Explain to the group that today they will be thinking about a sensitive topic: orgasms.

- Firstly, group members should think of ideas about what the word 'orgasm' means. Write ideas on a piece of flipchart paper.

- Group members should then pick a card and read it aloud to the group. Each card should be discussed. Can the cards be placed in a particular order?

- You may wish to print out a card sheet for each group member to keep in their private folder for reference.

- Finish with a fun and light-hearted game or activity.

Author note

The group may talk about different terms for orgasm, such as sexual excitement and semen. Refer back to Activity 11 where the group decided on terminology. Reinforce the importance of using the medically correct terms – this way language in future discussions will not be offensive and everyone will understand what is being talked about

Activity 38: The big O

What is an orgasm?

The feeling and reaction that happens when you are most sexually excited.

Why does it happen?

It happens when the private parts of the body are sexually excited by touch or sex.

What happens?

There are three parts. First is desire – we feel sexually attracted. Second is excitement – we feel sexually excited. Third is orgasm – when most sexually excited with an emotional and body reaction.

What is the body's reaction?

Your breathing gets quicker and your heart beats faster. Muscles around your private parts become tense. For men there is then a release of fluid from the penis. This is called semen.

What is the emotional reaction?

A release of tension and excitement. You may then feel calm, relaxed or even sleepy.

Afterwards ...

It takes a few minutes for your heart rate, temperature and breathing to return to normal. You may need to clean your private parts.

Activity 39: Masturbation musts

Preparation

You will need a piece of flipchart paper and a pen.

You will need to print and cut out the cards on the ideas sheets for the group to discuss.

You will need to print a copy of the worksheets and ideas sheets for each group member.

Instructions

- The group should sit in a circle with a table in the centre.

- Explain to the group that today they will be thinking about a sensitive topic: masturbation. Reassure the group that masturbation is a perfectly normal behaviour.

- Firstly, group members should work together to decide on a definition for masturbation. Be careful to only recommend reputable websites if group members are looking for ideas online. Ideally the group should come up with something along the lines of 'the stimulation or touch of your own genitals to feel good sexually or orgasm'.

- Next, take the 'What is masturbation?' cards from the ideas sheet and place them face down in the centre of the group. Group members should take it in turns to pick up a card, read it aloud and decide whether they feel this action is masturbation or not and discuss why.

- Group members should then complete an individual worksheet, using the ideas sheet if necessary to fill in appropriate ideas in the what, where, when and what happens boxes.

- Some of the options on the ideas sheet may never be OK. Discuss these with the group.

- If group members wish to feedback their worksheet at the end of the session that is fine but they don't need to as it is personal work.

- Finish with a fun and light-hearted game or activity.

Activity 39: Masturbation musts

Name .... Date ....

 What is masturbation?

Where?

Activity 39: Masturbation musts

 When?

 What happens?

Remember!

Masturbation is a normal human activity but must only done at an appropriate time and in an appropriate place. Afterwards you should clean yourself up if needed and put your clothes back on.

Let's talk about sex

Activity 39: Masturbation musts

Ideas Sheet

What is masturbation?	Touching 	Rubbing 	Touching 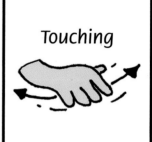
Hands in your pants 	Using sanitary products	Washing private parts	Scratching 
Rearranging underwear 	Wiping your bottom 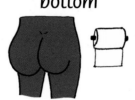	Fingering 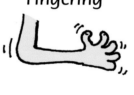	
Where could I masturbate?	At work 	On the bus 	In your bedroom 
In the bathroom 	In the public toilets	In the park 	At the cinema 

Activity 39: Masturbation musts

Ideas Sheet continued

In your partner's bedroom 	In your hotel room 	In a meeting	
When could I masturbate?	At night 	At mealtimes 	All the time 
At tea break 	In the shower 	In your free time **OFF DUTY!** 	
What happens?	You feel good 	You feel calm and relaxed 	You feel excited 
You feel bored 	You feel tired 	You feel embarrassed 	

Activity 40: Wet dreams

Preparation

You will need to print the story of William's wet dream. You may wish to laminate this if you will be using it again.

You will need a copy of the wet dreams cards and worksheet for each group member.

You will also need scissors and glue.

Instructions

- The group should sit around a table for this activity.

- Explain to the group that they will be doing an exercise around wet dreams today.

- Discuss with the group if anyone has heard the term before and what is means.

- Read the story of William's wet dream aloud to the group. Talk about what has happened and why. Do wet dreams only happen to men?

- Group members should now cut out their wet dreams cards and sort them into the correct order, revisiting the story of William's wet dream if necessary.

- Once happy their cards are in the correct order group members should stick them onto their worksheets.

- Group members can then put their worksheets into their private folders.

- Reinforce the message that wet dreams are a completely normal part of growing up.

Activity 40: Wet dreams

William's wet dream

William is a young man who likes rubgy, rock music and gaming.

William finishes his football game.

He goes to the bathroom, brushes his teeth and gets ready for bed.

William goes to sleep.

He dreams about someone he finds attractive.

William gets an erection – this means his penis becomes hard.

William's penis ejaculates – this means a liquid called semen shoots out.

William isn't aware of this because he is asleep.

In the morning, William wakes up.

William notices a damp patch around his penis.

William has tissues by his bed. He uses these to clean himself up.

William has a shower and puts his dirty clothes in the wash basket.

William gets dressed and is ready for the day.

All young men have wet dreams. It is normal and nothing to worry about.

Activity 40: Wet dreams

✂

 **Asleep**

 **Dreaming**

 **Gets an erection**

 **Ejaculates**

 **Wake up**

Activity 40: Wet dreams

 **Feel a damp patch**

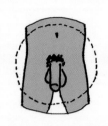 **Clean up**

 **Shower**

 **Ready for the day**

Name .... Date ....

```
┌──────────────────────────────────────────┐
│                                          │
│                                          │
│                                          │
└──────────────────────────────────────────┘
                    ↓
┌──────────────────────────────────────────┐
│                                          │
│                                          │
└──────────────────────────────────────────┘
                    ↓
┌──────────────────────────────────────────┐
│                                          │
│                                          │
└──────────────────────────────────────────┘
                    ↓
┌──────────────────────────────────────────┐
│                                          │
│                                          │
└──────────────────────────────────────────┘
                    ↓
┌──────────────────────────────────────────┐
│                                          │
│                                          │
└──────────────────────────────────────────┘
```

Activity 40: Wet dreams

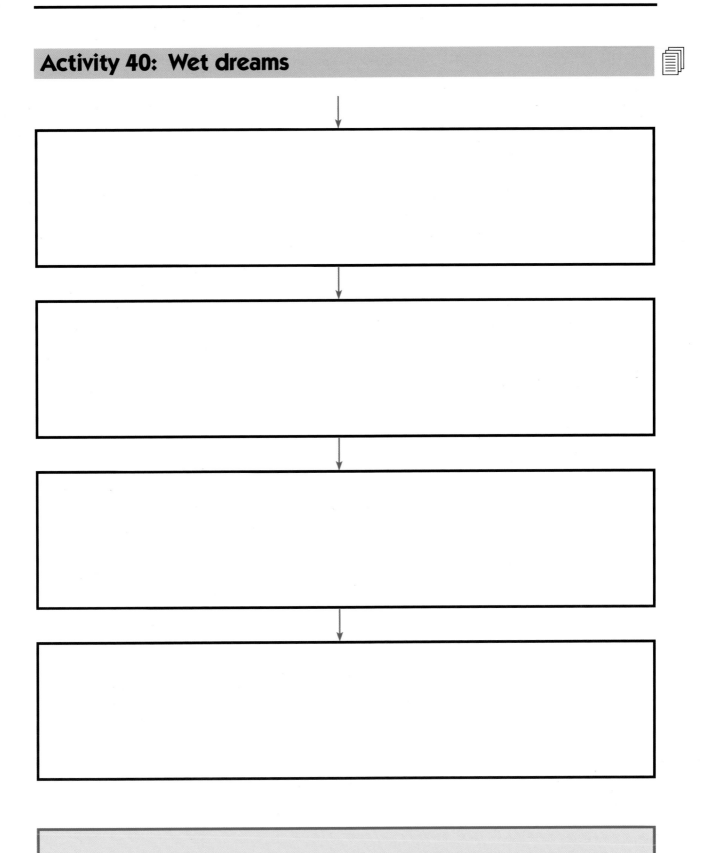

Remember: Wet dreams are normal and nothing to worry about!

Topic 4: Sex rules

Introduction

The aim of this topic is to help the group consider some of the difficulties surrounding having a sexual relationship. They first consider the crucial topic of consent, making sure they understand what this means and the importance of it. The group then explore the areas of peer pressure, the internet, pornography and public and private spaces. For each, the group complete activities to raise awareness and devise a plan to deal with these if needed.

Objectives
- To understand the importance of consent
- To consider some difficulties surrounding sexual relationships
- To know what is right and wrong
- To have some strategies to deal with these difficulties

Materials
- Print out and laminate activities as appropriate
- You will need Velcro™ to make up some of the activities
- Print out and photocopy worksheets as appropriate

Timing
- This topic will take up to 13 sessions to complete

Activity	Description
Consenting questions (Activity 41)	Using a number of silly question cards, the group ask and answer questions and consider what we mean by consent.
Comic of consent (Activity 42)	The group complete three comics, read each and decide if they are OK or not OK. They then discuss why one is not OK, because they didn't consent.
Ages around the world (Activity 43)	The group start by agreeing an appropriate definition for consent and discussing what this means. They then look up the age of consent in different countries around the world.
Am I ready? (Activity 44)	The group work through a set of questions considering at what stage in a relationship might it be OK to begin having sex, what you should do before you start and reinforcing that it is OK to say no and to change your mind.
Public or private? (Activity 45)	The group move around the room voting whether different places are public or private.
Where could I... (Activity 46)	Using the place cards from the previous activity, group members select an action card and match it to an appropriate place.
Peer pressure (Activity 47)	The group discuss what peer pressure means and where it comes from. They then read a story about Pete and consider the different pressures he faces and what he could do about them.
Internet safety (Activity 48)	The group read a number of scenarios and decide which option they should take if it was happening to them.
What is pornography? (Activity 49)	The group begin by agreeing an appropriate definition for pornography and then sort scenario cards into whether this is pornography or not.

 **Sex rules**

Activity	Description
Pornography quiz (Activity 50)	The group facilitator asks true or false questions about pornography and the group vote for which are real.
What could I do? (Activity 51)	Group members discuss three scenarios and consider what you should do if you suddenly felt unsafe in a situation.
Warning signs (Activity 52)	The group consider warning signs in relationships that might show it is unsafe or not going well. In two teams the group rate each situation.
Rules of relationships (Activity 53)	Group members discuss and devise rules around having a good and safe relationship.

Activity 41: Consenting questions

Preparation

You will need to print, laminate and cut out the consenting questions and then place them into a jar, or bag/box.

You will need a copy of the worksheet for each group member.

Instructions

- The group should sit in a circle.

- Explain to the group that today they will be asking each other questions.

- Pass around the jar or bag with the 'Consenting question' cards inside.

- Group members take it in turns to pick out a card and ask another member of the group the question. You may wish to encourage group members to ask the person sitting next to them or opposite them to ensure everyone will have a go at both asking and answering.

- Some of the questions will sound silly but encourage group members to try to answer them as sensibly as possible.

- Once everyone has had a go at both asking and answering a question, discuss as a group how they felt. Did people understand what they were being asked? Would we ever agree/consent to doing something that we didn't fully understand? How can we appropriately say no?

- Group members can now read, discuss and keep the worksheet on consent. This could also be enlarged to A3 and displayed on the wall in the room where the group meet if appropriate

Activity 41: Consenting questions

Ask someone to shout out something rude.

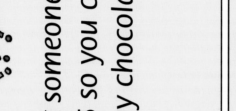

Ask someone for £5 so you can buy chocolate.

Ask someone to look after your gadoodle for five minutes.

Ask someone if you can touch their noggin.

Ask someone for a gobgoobler.

Ask someone to show you their plushpopper.

Ask to borrow someone's phone to call your mum.

Ask someone for their lunch because you haven't got any.

Activity 41: Consenting questions

Name: .... Date: ....

Consent means...

 **You have been asked**
respectfully by the other person

 **You understand**
exactly what the other person is asking you to do

 **You want to do it**
You also want to do what the person is
suggesting, you are not just agreeing because
you are scared to say no.

Activity 42: Comic of consent

Preparation

Print all three worksheets, enlarge to A3, and laminate them.

You will also need a thin dry wipe pen to write on the worksheets.

Instructions

- In the previous two activities the group would have started the topic of consent.

- Explain to the group that they will be looking at the topic of consent in more detail today and in three different scenarios.

- The group facilitator should start with 'Comic of consent … take one'. The group should discuss and fill in the character's thoughts (bubbles) and feelings (hearts) at each stage.

- Ask the group how they feel about the story: is it OK or not OK?

- Now the group should complete 'Comic of consent … take two' and discuss how important it is to listen to your partner and respect their wishes.

- Continue with 'Comic of consent … take three'. Discuss with the group how you would feel if someone ignored you and made you do something you did not want to do.

- Three themes should emerge from the activity: story one will always be OK because the couple are consenting. Story two will always be OK because one character has said they don't want to do something and the other person has listened and respected their decision. Story three is never OK: we should never make someone else do something they don't want to.

Activity 42: Comic of consent... take one

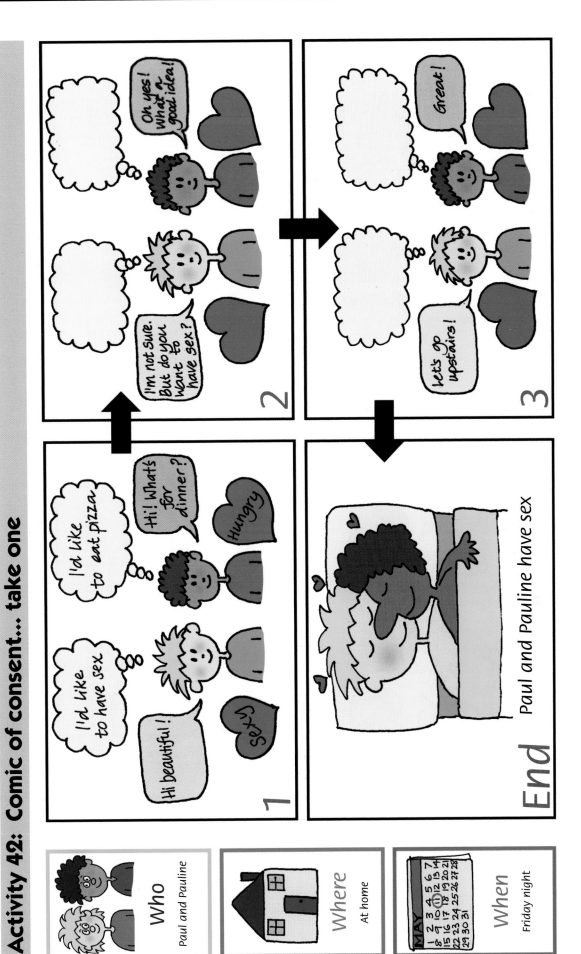

Activity 42: Comic of consent... take two

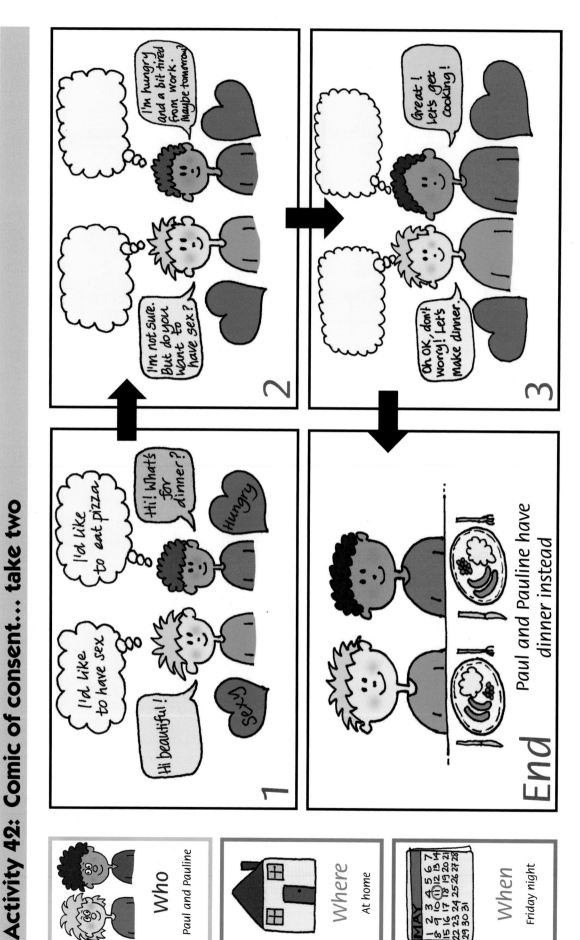

Who — Paul and Pauline

Where — At home

When — Friday night

1
- *I'd like to have sex*
- Hi beautiful!
- *I'd like to eat pizza*
- Hi! What's for dinner?

2
- I'm not sure. But do you want to have sex?
- I'm hungry and a bit tired from work. Maybe tomorrow?

3
- Oh OK, don't worry! Let's make dinner.
- Great! Let's get cooking!

End — Paul and Pauline have dinner instead

Activity 42: Comic of consent... take three

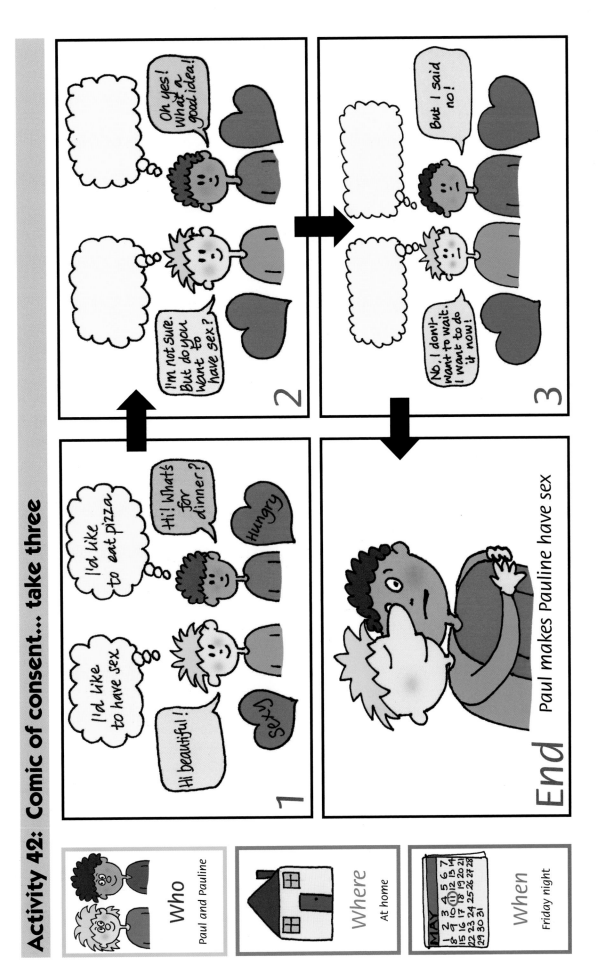

Activity 43: Ages around the world

Preparation

You will need to print and enlarge the 'Ages around the world' worksheet to A3. You may wish to laminate this and use a dry wipe pen if you will be using it again.

If you are doing this as an individual activity you will need to print a copy for each group member (A3 still works best).

Instructions

• The group should be seated around a table for this activity.

• Explain to the group that they will be starting a new topic looking at the rules around sex. Today they will be learning about the age of consent and how this changes around the world.

• First, ask the group if anyone knows what 'age of consent' means? Group members could then look up a definition online or in a dictionary and agree as a group what this means. This can then be written on the bottom of the worksheet.

• Group members should then research the age of consent in each of the different counties highlighted. You may like to split the group into teams or pairs to do this.

• When everyone has finished, spend a bit of time feeding back the different ages. Are they all the same or are some different? Which is the youngest? Which is the oldest? Are there any we have found particularly interesting?

• The group should then add their country and the age of consent in the bubble at the bottom.

Author note: *at time of publication the ages of consent were as follows: UK 16, Italy 14, Canada 16, Ireland 17, China 14, Argentina 18, Angola 12, Bahrain 21, Fiji 16.*

Activity 43: Ages around the world

Name: ....

Date: ....

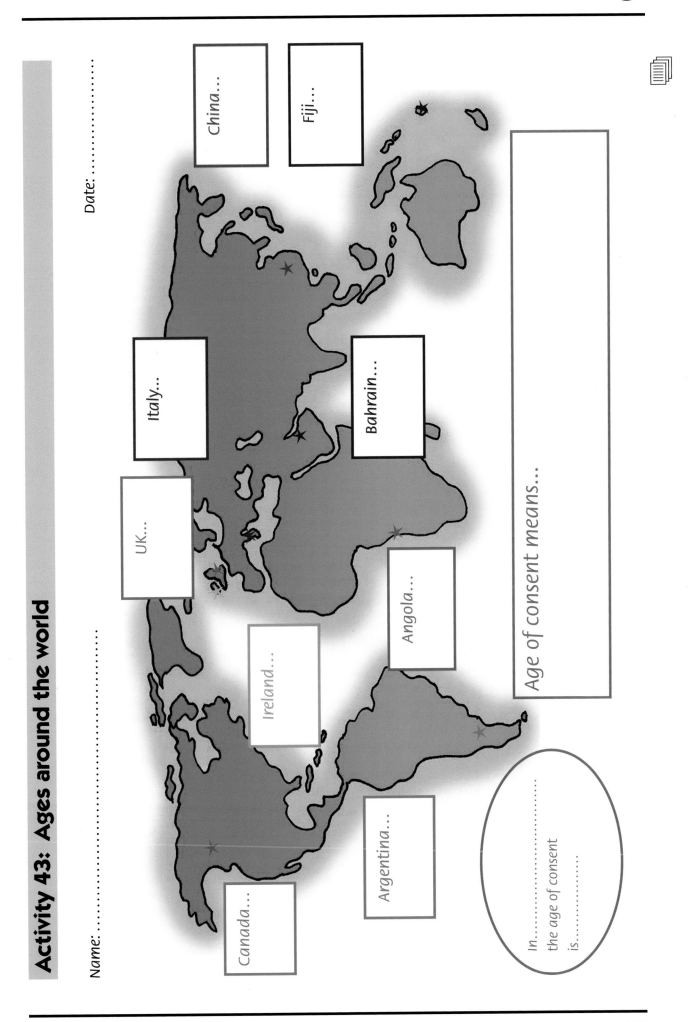

China...

Fiji...

Italy...

Bahrain...

UK...

Angola...

Ireland...

Argentina...

Canada...

Age of consent means....

In................
the age of consent
is................

Activity 44: Am I ready?

Preparation

You will need to print out a copy of the worksheet for each group member.

Instructions

- Introduce the session by telling the group that they will be thinking about a subject that is more personal today - how do we know if we are ready for a sexual relationship? Check the group understand this term and are all comfortable to continue.

- Ask the group what stage in a relationship would be right to begin a sexual relationship. Are there any times where it would not be appropriate at all, for example when people first meet? Discuss the group's ideas and opinions.

- Group members should write on the stage/time, when the group agreed it would be appropriate to begin a sexual relationship if they want to into the top box of their worksheets.

- Next discuss as a group what a couple should do before they begin having sex; for example both must consent, you must feel comfortable, talk it through or say how you feel, etc. Write these into the second box.

- Discuss the 'REMEMBER!' statement and reinforce the message that it is important to stay safe and only agree to having sex if you want to.

- Lastly discuss as a group what you should do if you are not ready to start having sex or change your mind after agreeing. The group should think about saying 'no' assertively, talking to their partner, saying how they feel and explaining their decision/reasons.

- If group members prefer, they could complete the sheets individually first and then share ideas as a group if they feel comfortable to.

Variation

If you have used Talkabout Sex & Relationships Volume 1 you may like to revisit Activity 43 'Love grows' to see how relationships grow and develop over time.

Activity 44: Am I ready?

A sexual relationship

Name ....   Date ....

> When? **?**
>
> ....

> What should we do when we think we are ready? **?**
> -
> -
> -
> -

REMEMBER! ⟩ It is OK to change your mind

> What should we do if we are not ready? **?**
> -
> -
> -
> -

Activity 45: Public or Private?

Preparation

Print, laminate and cut out the places cards.

You will also need to print, laminate and cut out the 'Public' and 'Private' heading cards.

Instructions

- Attach the 'Public' and 'Private' heading cards onto opposite walls of the room.

- Encourage all group members to stand up as they will be moving around for this activity.

- Group members take it in turns to pick up a place card and read it aloud.

- Group members should move between the two sides of the room depending on whether they feel this is a public or private place.

- If there are any differences in opinion in the group, allow discussion after each card.

- Discuss how we know if somewhere is public or private. Does it affect what we are able to do in that place?

Variation

If the group would prefer to stay seated, put the place cards in the centre of the circle face down in a pile. Group members should then take it in turns to pick a card and place it under the 'public' and 'private' headings.

Activity 45: Public or Private?

✂

Public

Private

At College

In the town centre

Activity 45: Public or Private?

In the toilet at home 	In the bathroom at home 
In my bedroom 	In my partner's bedroom 
In public toilets 	In my friend's bedroom 

Activity 45: Public or Private?

In the toilet at work 	At work 
In the living room 	At a friend's house 
In the Doctors room 	At a Day Service 

Activity 45: Public or Private?

In the changing room	In the park

On the bus	At church

At the dentist	At the swimming pool

Activity 45: Public or Private?

✂

At the supermarket	At the beach

In a restaurant	At a pub
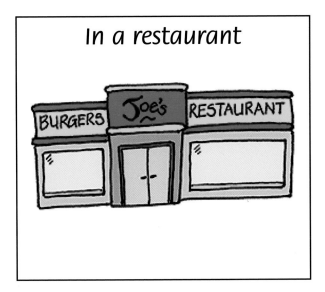	
At the gym	At the cinema

Activity 46: Where could I ....

Preparation

You will need the place cards from Activity 45.

You will need to print, laminate and cut out the 'Where could I …' cards. You may wish to put these in a jar or a hat.

Instructions

- The group should sit in a circle.

- Lay out the place cards on the floor in the middle of the group. The group may wish to add some of their own.

- Pass around the jar or hat with the 'Where could I …' cards inside.

- Group members take it in turns to pick out a card and read it aloud to the group. You may wish to warn the group that some of these are quite personal.

- The group member then matches the 'Where could I …' card to an appropriate place card and says why they feel this would be OK.

- Discuss any differences in opinion with the group. Are any other places where this would be appropriate?

Additional Activity

Group members could make their own 'Where could I …' cards and match them to places where these would be appropriate.

Activity 46: Where could I ....

 Be naked

Get dressed

Get undressed

 Change sanitary products

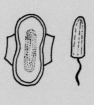 Kiss

 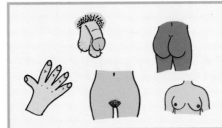 Touch private parts

 Have sex

 Hold hands

 Go to sleep

 Hug

 Watch pornography

 Masturbate

Activity 46: Where could I ....

 Check for lumps

 Talk about private things

 Chat

 Eat

 Fart

 Burp

Sex rules

Activity 47: Peer pressure

Preparation

You will need to print a copy of the different types of peer pressure for each group member.

Print out the story of Pete. You may wish to laminate this if you will be using it again.

You will need to print a copy of the table in A4 for individual work or enlarge to A3 if this will be done as a group activity.

You may also need paper and pens to write down ideas.

Instructions

- The group should sit around a table for this activity.

- Explain to the group that they will be doing an exercise around peer pressure today. Has anyone heard of it before? You may wish to discuss some ideas and come up with a definition.

- Discuss where they think peer pressure comes from. Is it always from other people? Talk about how it can sometimes come from within you. Look at the worksheet and consider the differences. Can they think of an example for each one?

- The facilitator should then read Pete's story to the group. After, the group members discuss what happened and consider the examples of peer pressure Pete faces and what he should do, filling out the table.

- Read through the 'Remember!' statement and discuss as a group.

Activity 47: Peer pressure

Name ....

Date ....

Where does peer pressure come from?

1

Directly...
You may experience peer pressure when someone tells you what you should be doing. For example, how to spend your time, how to behave and things you should try.

2

Indirectly...
You may not always recognise peer pressure but you may find that you behave in a certain way with a particular group of friends. This means they are having an indirect effect on you.

3

From you...
Sometimes the pressure comes from inside you. You may feel like you are different from your friends and do things to make yourself feel like you are part of the group.

Remember! Peer pressure is not always a bad thing. Sometimes our peers pressure us to behave in a better way and this can have a positive effect on us.

Activity 47: Peer pressure

Pete's story

Pete is 20, he likes going to the cinema and enjoys reading history books, especially about ancient Eygpt.

Pete is a virgin – this means he has not had sex before. He has been in a relationship with Polly for six months. They get on well and have lots of things in common.

Recently, Polly has told Pete she would like to have sex with him. Pete is worried as he doesn't feel ready yet and thinks they should get to know each other better.

On Saturday, Pete takes Polly out for dinner to their favourite restruant. Pete wants to tell Polly that he loves her for the first time and is really excited. After their starter he plucks up the courage to do it.

> Polly, I'm in love with you!

> Oh Pete! I love you too!

Pete is very pleased, things are going really well with Polly.

> Would you like to stay at my house tonight?

> Umm maybe... I haven't got my pyjamas though.

Activity 47: Peer pressure

That's OK, we should sleep naked. All couples do!

Do they? I don't know if I want to...

But you said you loved me!

I do Polly, I just don't feel ready.

You would do it if you **really** loved me!

You are just being mean!

After a big argument Pete goes home feeling very sad. That wasn't the meal he had planned. Maybe he should just do it?

At college on Monday Pete is feeling happier and having fun with his friends. He asks his friend James what he got up to at the weekend.

Oh it was amazing! I hooked up with this fit girl!

Really? How was it? What was it like?

Activity 47: Peer pressure

It was great! You have to do it mate!

I just don't think I'm ready yet.

You're a 20 year old man! Of course you are ready!

I've been doing it for years, you're weird!

After a rubbish day at college, Pete goes home and tries to cheer himself up by watching his favourite TV soap. He can't help thinking maybe he is weird?

On the TV it seems like everyone is having sex, even the new character who is 18!

Am I normal? Am I strange? If everyone else is doing it then what's wrong with me?

Me?

FINE! I'll just do it!

Activity 47: Peer pressure

Name ....   Date ....

The pressures	Type of pressure? (Direct, indirect, from you)	What should Pete do?
"You would do it if you <u>really</u> loved me!"		
"You are just being mean!"		
"You are a 20 year old man! Of course you are ready!"		
"I've been doing it for years, you're weird!"		
Everyone is having sex on TV, even the 18 year olds.		
Am I normal? Am I strange? If everyone else is doing it then what's wrong with me?		

Remember!

You should never be pressured into anything you don't want to do!

You always have a choice and can change your mind!

Sex rules

Activity 48: Internet Safety

Preparation

Print out all the cards; these are best printed on card. To make them up take the left-hand number card and stick it back to back with the right-hand A, B, C option card. You may wish to laminate these if you will be using them again.

You may also like to make up A, B and C voting cards or use mini whiteboards for the group to vote with.

Instructions

- The group should sit around a table for this activity.

- Tell the group that they will be doing an exercise around internet safety today.

- Explain that you will read through several scenarios and after each one group members should vote for the correct response.

- Discuss each card as a group before moving onto the next scenario.

- You may find some common themes emerging such as 'tell someone you trust'. You may wish to re-visit Activity 8, to look at the top three people we trust in our own lives.

Activity 48: Internet Safety

1.

You get a friend request from someone you do not know.
Should you …

A. Accept the friend request

B. Ignore them and decline the request

C. Ask them for more information to prove they know you

2.

An ex-partner contacts you to say they have a photo of you naked.
Should you …

A. Tell someone you trust

B. Post rude photos of them online

C. Do nothing

3.

You click on a website and discover sexual images that upset you.
Should you …

A. Continue browsing the website

B. Share the link with all your friends

C. Close the page immediately and tell someone you trust

Activity 48: Internet Safety

4.

You've been chatting to someone on an online game, they suggest meeting up.
Should you …

A. Agree and suggest a time and place

B. Talk to someone you trust before making a decision

C. Call them a rude name for suggesting it

5.

You have recently been on holiday with your friend and want to upload a photo of you both in your swimwear at the beach.
Should you…

A. Upload and tag your friend

B. Upload the photo but don't tell your friend, it might upset them

C. Ask your friend's permission before sharing the photo

6.

You open a new app you have downloaded and it asks you to share your location.
Should you …

A. Skip this step, don't locate yourself

B. Share your location, the app looks like it will be fun

C. Go to a local café and share that location rather than your home

Activity 49: What is pornography?

Preparation

You will need to print and cut out the yes / no cards and statement cards. You may wish to laminate these if they will be used again.

You may also need some pens and a piece of flipchart paper.

Instructions

- The group should sit around a table for this activity.

- Explain to the group that they will be doing an exercise around the subject of pornography today.

- Ask group members if they have heard the term pornography before. What does it mean? You may wish to add ideas to a piece of flipchart paper.

- Introduce the sorting activity. Place the yes / no cards on the table. Group members then take it in turns to take a statement card, read it aloud and decide whether 'yes', this is pornography or 'no', this is not. Discuss each one as a group.

- You may wish to finish with a lighthearted game or activity if anyone has become anxious or uncomfortable.

Additional activity

You may wish to write your own scenarios to add to the sorting activity.

Activity 49: What is pornography?

Yes	NO

A family photo of you and your brother or sister playing in a paddling pool naked as children

A couple kissing in a music video

A sex scene in a film

Accidently leaving the door unlocked and someone walking in while you are showering

A magazine containing images of people doing different sexual acts

A website showing videos of people doing different sexual acts

Activity 50: Pornography quiz

Preparation

You will need the 'true' or 'false' voting cards from Activity 18. Print out a copy of the quiz.

You will need a copy of the worksheet for each group member.

You may also need some pens and piece of flipchart paper.

Instructions

- The group should sit around a table for this activity.

- Explain to the group that they will be talking more about the subject of pornography today.

- Hand out the 'true' or 'false' voting cards from Activity 18. Read out the questions one at a time then ask group members to vote on whether they think it is true or false and discuss.

- Lastly, hand out a copy of the worksheet to each group member. They should complete the worksheet considering the things they have learnt in the quiz and previous activity. They can either come up with their own definition or use the Oxford English Dictionary definition which is:

'Printed or visual material containing the explicit description or display of sexual organs or activity intended to stimulate sexual excitement.' (2017)

- Finish with a light-hearted game or activity.

Additional activity

Statistics around pornography change all the time. You may wish to look up some of your own to discuss alongside the quiz.

You may also wish to revisit Activity 39 'Masturbation musts' to think about when and where it would be appropriate to watch pornography.

 **Activity 50: Pornography quiz**

Quiz

1. Everyone watches pornography.

2. The sex shown in pornography is 'normal'.

3. Most pornography is viewed on computers.

4. Any pornography containing images of children is illegal.

5. Porn stars' bodies look like the average person's body.

Answers

1. False! Some people watch pornography, some people don't. This includes both men and women, in relationships and single, of all sexualities and of different ages.

2. False! The sex shown in pornography is exaggerated and extreme; it does not represent the type of sex people have in happy, healthy relationships.

3. False! The majority of pornography is now viewed on mobile devices like smart phones and tablets.

4. True! Any pornography containing images of people under 18 years of age is illegal.

5. False! Porn stars have often had cosmetic surgery to make them look the way they do. Breasts and penis sizes are often enlarged as well as little or no pubic hair. This does not represent the average person.

Activity 50: Pornography quiz

Name . . . .   Date . . . .

Pornography is …

The rules are …

Remember …

 ## Activity 51: What could I do?

Preparation

You will need to print an ideas sheet, either in A3 for the whole group to work on or in A4 for individual work.

You will also need a copy of the worksheet for each group member.

Instructions

• The group should sit around a table for this activity.

• Explain to the group that today they will be thinking about what you might do if a situation became unsafe.

• Either individually or as a group, consider ideas of what we could do if we felt unsafe in a situation such as:

Say 'No'	Take time out
Talk to someone	Ask for help
Think	Count to 10
Say how you feel	Call the police

• The group should then read the three scenarios and think about good (green), OK (amber) and bad (red) ideas for each.

• Group members can then feed back their ideas and discuss as a group.

Activity 51: What could I do?

Name: ....

Date: ....

What could I do if I feel unsafe?

 Activity 51: What could I do?

Name: ....   Date: ....

You are walking your dog in the local park. A stranger approaches and asks if you would like to have a look at their new puppy in the back of their car.		
You are at a disco, dancing with your friends. One of your friends gives you a hug and tries to kiss you. You feel uncomfortable and do not want to do this.		
You are in the car with your support worker. They reach over and stroke your leg. You do not like it.		

Activity 52: Warning signs

Preparation

You will need to print, cut out and enlarge the cards then stick them around the room.

You will also need to print and cut out the warning symbols. Attach a piece of sticky tac to the back of each.

You may wish to laminate these resources if you will be using them more than once.

Instructions

- The group should sit in a circle.

- Explain to the group that today they will be thinking about the potential warning signs that we may notice in relationships.

- Split the group into two teams and give each group several warning symbols.

- Explain to the two teams that they will be going around the room, reading the different scenarios and deciding on whether or not they feel this may be a potential warning sign.

- If the team feel the scenario may be potentially risky / unsafe they should attach a warning sign to it.

- Once both teams have finished looking at all the scenarios the group should come back together and discuss their findings as a larger group. You may wish to collate a list on a piece of flipchart paper.

- Group members should now complete their warning signs summary sheet and once completed add this to their individual work folders.

 **Sex rules**

Activity 52: Warning signs

Your partner is 20 years older than you, you do not have much in common.	Your partner is unemployed and shown no interest in looking for a job. They use the money you earn to go clothes shopping and for days out with their friends.
Your partner wants to have sex every night of the week. When you don't want to they make you feel guilty and say you would do it if you loved them.	Whenever you go out with your partner they flirt with other people, they say they are just being friendly but it makes you feel embarrassed and jealous.
Your partner keeps taking your phone and reading your messages. The other day they got angry at you and accused you of flirting with a work colleague.	You and your partner got into a heated argument last week. They screamed in your face and pushed you.

Activity 52: Warning signs

Your partner does not like your family, they are rude about them and do not like you spending any time with them.

Your partner always makes nasty comments about your appearance, they make you wear baggy, old clothes as they say you are getting chubby.

You and your partner have an argument about where to go for dinner, they call you selfish as you always choose the restaurant and won't listen to any of their suggestions.

You don't have a lot in common with your partner but you always get on well and make each other happy.

Your partner suggests you wear your hair in a certain way as it really suits you and makes you look beautiful.

Your partner is a big football fan and spends evenings and weekends playing and watching their favourite team. You wish they would spend more time with you.

Activity 52: Warning signs

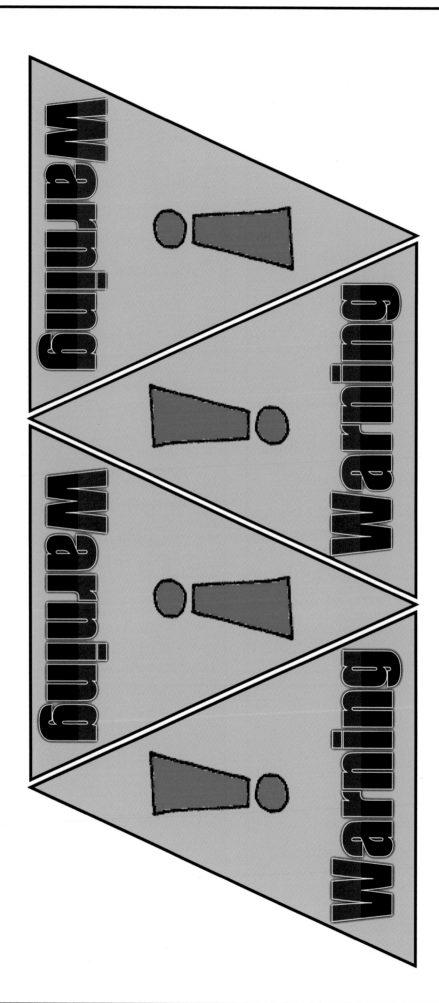

Activity 52: Warning signs

Name: .... Date: ....

If I spotted a warning sign in my relationship I could…

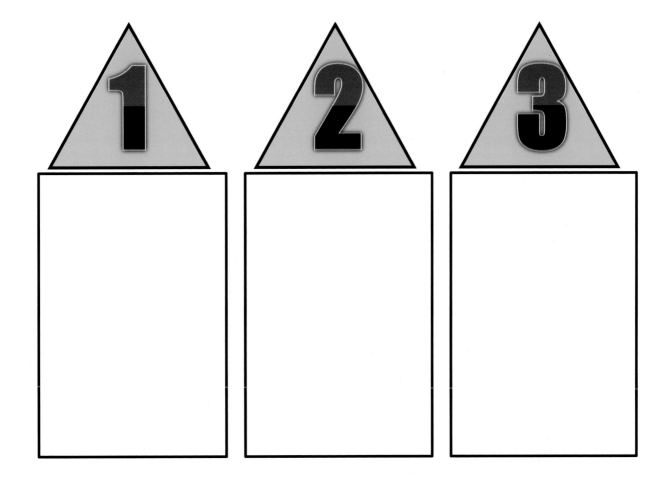

 **Sex rules**

Activity 53: Rules of relationships

Preparation

Print out worksheets for each group member in A4 or enlarge to A3 for a whole group activity.

Instructions

- Ask the group to create rules around having a good relationship.

- They should come up with the ideas themselves but the group facilitator should guide them to include the following:

  1. You must both be over 16.

  2. You must never do anything you feel uncomfortable with.

  3. You must never make a partner do anything they feel uncomfortable with.

  4. You should only have one partner at a time (a monogamous relationship)

  5. It is better to already be friends with someone before you start a relationship.

- Discuss why these rules are important.

- Group members can then place their rules into their private work folder.

Activity 53: Rules of relationships

Name: .... Date: ....

Rules of relationships

-

-

-

-

-

Remember ...

 Topic 5: Sex aware

Introduction

The aim of this topic is to look at staying safe and also the possible consequences of having sexual intercourse. The group begin by exploring what contraception is, what is available and the pros and cons for each. They then consider what pregnancy is, what happens and what the choices are if you find out you are expecting. Finally this topic covers STIs and sexual health, again raising awareness of what these are and what can be done to help.

Objectives
- To understand what contraception means and know what choices are available
- To understand what pregnancy is
- To know what STIs are and their symptoms
- To have some ideas of what to do to maintain good sexual health

Materials
- Print out and laminate activities as appropriate
- You will need Velcro™ to make up some of the activities
- Print out and photocopy worksheets as appropriate

Timing
- This topic will take up to 8 sessions to complete

Activity	Description
Contraception (Activity 54)	The group begin by agreeing an appropriate definition for what contraception is and then create a list of all the different types used currently including pros and cons for each.
Pregnancy puns (Activity 55)	Using a set of cards, the group consider different words people say to mean pregnancy and then sort them into 'slang terms', 'old-fashioned terms' and 'correct terms'.
What is pregnancy? (Activity 56)	The group order a set of cards to show what happens at each stage of pregnancy.
Charlie's choice (Activity 57)	The group read about Charlie and the three decisions she has following finding out she is pregnant. Group members discuss the pros and cons for each and decide what she could do.
STIs (Activity 58)	The group discuss what STI means and then create a list of different STIs including their symptoms and how they are treated. The group also consider what they should do if they think they might have an STI.
What is sexual health? (Activity 59)	Group members discuss what is meant by sexual health and create a list of all the different areas within that.
Speaking up for sexual health (Activity 60)	This final activity gets the group to plan what they could do if they needed support with their sexual health, where could they go and whom could they talk to.
Certificates	Certificates for each group member to celebrate their achievements and the end of the course.

 **Sex aware**

Activity 54: Contraception

Preparation

You will need to print a copy of the 'Contraception is ...' worksheet for each group member and 16 copies of the 'pros and cons' worksheet.

Enlarge the 'Different forms of contraception' sheet to A3. If you will be using this more than once, laminate the board and a set of the individual contraception squares and then use Velcro™ to attach these squares to the board so that they can be taken off separately.

Instructions

- The group should sit around a table for this activity.

- Explain to the group that today they will be thinking about contraception.

- Ask group members if they have heard of contraception before. What does it mean? Why do people use it? You may wish to write down ideas on a piece of paper as a group.

- Group members should then decide on a definition and add this to their 'Contraception is ...' worksheet. They could use a dictionary or look up ideas online.

- Next, group members should take it in turns to think of different types of contraception.

- Use the 'Different contraception' board. Have the individual squares in a separate bag if you have made these up. Each time a group member correctly identifies a method of contraception, give them the square to attach to the board.

- Group members then work in pairs or small groups to research different methods of contraception in more detail, using the 'pros and cons' worksheet to gather relevant information. Give each group/pair 1 or 2 to research.

- You may wish to have a number of leaflets explaining each type for the group to use in this activity.

- Once all methods have been researched, the pairs then feed back their research to the rest of the group.

Activity 54: Contraception

Name .... Date ....

Contraception is ...

Sex aware

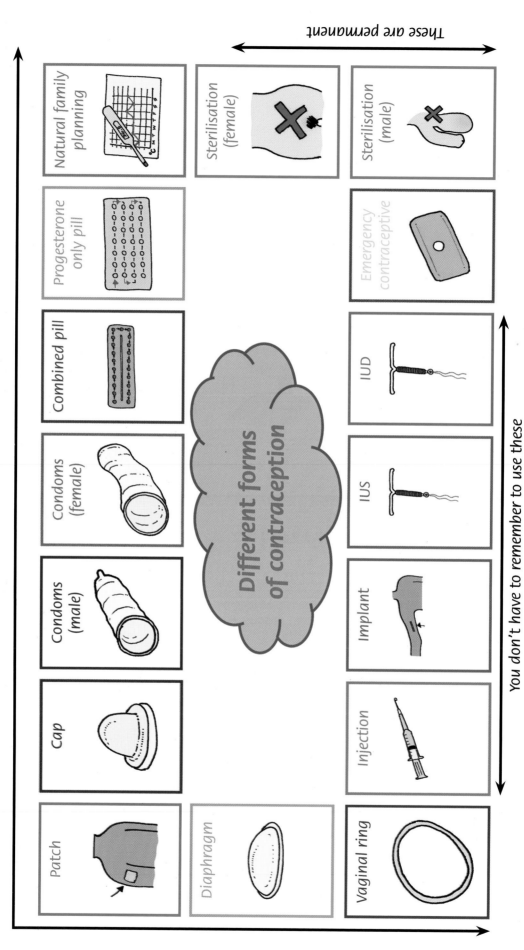

These are permanent

You need to remember to use these

These can be used in an emergency

You don't have to remember to use these

Natural family planning

Sterilisation (female)

Sterilisation (male)

Progesterone only pill

Emergency contraceptive

Combined pill

IUD

Condoms (female)

IUS

Condoms (male)

Different forms of contraception

Implant

Cap

Injection

Patch

Diaphragm

Vaginal ring

Activity 54: Contraception

Name: .... Date: ....

Method of contraception:

✓ ☐ ✗

Pros

_____

_____

_____

_____

_____

_____

_____

_____

Cons

_____

_____

_____

_____

_____

_____

_____

_____

Protection against STIs

(✓ or ✗) ☐

 ## Activity 55: Pregnancy puns

Preparation

You will need to print and cut out the 'pregnancy puns'. You may wish to laminate these if you will be using them more than once. You will also need the category cards from Activity 34.

You may like to use a piece of flipchart paper and pens to write down ideas.

Instructions

- The group should sit around a table for this activity.

- Group members discuss what the word 'pregnancy' means, adding ideas to a piece of flipchart paper.

- The facilitator should then re-introduce the three categories 'Correct terms', 'old-fashioned' and 'Slang' from Activity 34, recapping what they mean.

- The group members then take it in turns to pick a 'pregnancy puns' card, read it aloud and decide which category it fits into.

- You may wish to add additional ideas the group came up with while discussing pregnancy at the start of the session and sort these too.

- Discuss with the group why it is important to use the correct terms. This way we know that we won't upset people by using offensive language and everyone will understand what we are discussing.

Activity 55: Pregnancy puns

A bun in the oven

Having a baby

Expecting

Up the duff

With child

Knocked up

Preggers

Prego

Eating for two

In the family way

Carrying a child

 **Sex aware**

 ## Activity 56: What is pregnancy?

Preparation

You will need to print the pregnancy cards, stick the corresponding information and picture card back to back, and laminate.

Instructions

- The group should sit around a table for this activity.

- Explain to the group that they will be looking at pregnancy in more detail today.

- Muddle up the cards and place them, picture side up, on the table. Ask the group to work together to put the cards in the right order.

- When this is done, turn the cards over, read the information and swap any around that are out of place.

- Talk through the different stages of pregnancy – as the baby grows the woman's body changes.

- Depending on the group members' ability you might discuss conception and birth in more detail. You may wish to use additional resources such as videos to help explain what happens at these stages.

- You may also wish to discuss that pregnancy doesn't always go to plan:

  o Sometimes people get pregnant by accident – perhaps the contraception they are using doesn't work.

  o Some people get pregnant the first time they have sex, others can spend years trying to get pregnant. Sometimes people are unable to get pregnant and might choose to adopt a baby.

  o Sometimes a woman has a miscarriage. This means the baby dies before it is ready to be born. It still comes out of the woman's vagina but is not alive. This happens quite a lot and could be for many reasons.

  o Sometimes the baby grows to full size but dies. The woman still has to give birth to the baby but it is not alive.

  o Sometimes babies need help to be born. Women may need a caesarean section. The woman has an operation to help the baby out of her tummy.

- You may wish to finish the session by sharing stories of when siblings or family members were born. You could talk about how tiny they were and how group members may have felt to have a new baby in the family. Alternatively you could ask group members to bring in photographs of themselves as a baby.

Activity 56: What is pregnancy?

What is pregnancy?

Pregnancy is when a baby is growing in a woman's tummy.

It starts from a tiny fertilised egg (the size of a grain of sand) and grows to the size of a newborn baby.

Pregnancy lasts around 40 weeks.

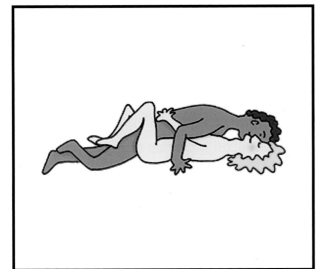

Conception

When a man and a woman have sexual intercourse the man's penis releases semen which contains lots of tiny sperm into the woman's vagina. If one of these sperm meets an egg from the woman's ovaries the egg will start growing into a baby.

1st Trimester

Weeks 1 – 12

The fertilised egg develops into an embryo and then into a foetus. By the end of week 12 all the baby's muscles, bones and organs have formed. Some women have 'morning sickness' at this stage of pregnancy.

Activity 56: What is pregnancy?

2nd Trimester

Weeks 13 -28

In the second trimester women often start to 'feel' more pregnant, morning sickness goes and they have more energy. This is when their 'bump' starts to grow and they feel their baby move for the first time.

3rd Trimester

Weeks 29 – 40

The baby continues to grow until it's ready to be born. It changes position, from head facing up to head facing down, ready for the birth. The woman should try to get as much rest as she can as a newborn baby is very tiring!

Birth

When the baby is ready to be born the woman's waters will break and she will start having contractions. This can take a long time and is often tiring and painful. Finally she pushes the baby out of her vagina and into the world.

Activity 57: Charlie's choice

Preparation

You will need to enlarge the story to A3 if you will be doing this as a group activity or print each member a copy if they will be working on it individually.

You may wish to laminate it and use dry wipe pens if using it again.

You will also need to print a copy of the ideas sheet for each group member.

Instructions

• The group should sit around a table for this activity.

• Refer back to the previous activities around contraception and pregnancy. Explain to the group that as they have found out, contraception isn't always reliable and people can get pregnant without trying for a baby.

• Read the story to the group, pausing to allow time for group members to complete the written section. You may wish to use books or reputable websites to help the group generate ideas.

• Once you have finished the story, discuss the three choices Charlie now has. What are the group's ideas and opinions on each? You may wish to talk about how values, opinions and sometimes religion or the law might affect people's decisions. Ultimately there is no right or wrong answer; it is the person's individual decision.

• Next, group members should complete the ideas sheet considering things that might help Charlie make her choice. These could include talking to Oscar, talking to a close friend or family member, researching each option to be able to make an informed choice, considering how each option may affect her life in the future.

• Finish the session with a light-hearted game or activity.

Activity 57: Charlie's choice

Name: .... Date: ....

Charlie is a young woman who is hoping to start college in September. She loves animals, especially horses and riding her Pony Reggie. She is really excited about the future and dreams of becoming a vet one day.

Charlie has been dating Oscar who lives down the road. They enjoy spending time together and have had sex but neither wants a serious relationship at the moment. Oscar is also leaving to go travelling soon; they will remain friends but nothing more.

However, Charlie thinks she might be pregnant. She has missed her period and has been feeling really tired as well as having bad back ache.

How could Charlie find out if she is definitely pregnant?
• ....
• ....
• ....

When the tests come back as positive Charlie knows for sure that she is pregnant. She starts thinking, what are the options?

Charlie's doctor gives her a leaflet, it explains the different options available. There are three.

1. To keep the baby

2. To have an abortion

3. To have the baby adopted

Activity 57: Charlie's choice

Name .... Date ....

1. To have the baby

This means..

....

Pros

1.
2.
3.

Cons

1.
2.
3.

2. To have an abortion

This means..

....

Pros

1.
2.
3.

Cons

1.
2.
3.

3. To have the baby adopted

This means..

....

Pros

1.
2.
3.

Cons

1.
2.
3.

Activity 57: Charlie's choice

Name: ....

Date: ....

What could Charlie do to help her make the right choice?

Activity 58: STIs

Preparation

You will need to print a copy of the worksheet (both pages) for each group member.

You may also need a piece of flipchart paper and pens.

Instructions

- The group should sit around a table for this activity.

- Explain to the group that they will be doing an exercise around STIs today.

- Ask group members if they have heard this term before. What does it stand for? Can anyone think of any examples of different STIs? Write any ideas on a piece of flipchart paper.

- Hand out a copy of the worksheet to each group member. They can either work on this individually or split into pairs to look up information together. You may wish to use books, leaflets or reputable websites.

- Group members should then feed back ideas as part of the larger group, discuss their findings and add any extra STIs to their worksheets.

- Talk though the 'If you think you have an STI' box at the bottom of the worksheet as a group. It might be useful to refer back to Activity 27: Helpful health, to remind the group of the local sexual health clinic.

 ## Activity 58: STIs

Name: ....   Date: ....

What does it mean?

STI

S...

T...

I ....

S T why? How do people get them?

....

....

STI	Symptoms	Treatment

Activity 58: STIs

STI	Symptoms	Treatment

If you think you might have an STI …

- Go to the doctor or to your nearest sexual health clinic – they will test to see if you have an STI.

- Tell previous sexual partners as they may also have the STI and will need to be treated themselves.

Sex aware

Activity 59: What is sexual health?

Preparation

You will need to enlarge the ideas sheet to A3.

If you will be using this more than once you may wish to print two copies, laminate one copy then cut out the different headings from the other, laminate and Velcro™ them onto the first sheet so each heading can be removed separately.

Instructions

- Group members should sit around a table for this activity.

- Explain that this week we will be looking at sexual health services in more detail.

- Group members should discuss what sexual health is and then take it in turns to think of different parts of sexual health.

- Each time a group member correctly identifies an area, give them the corresponding heading which they can attach to the ideas sheet.

- Discuss each area and think of different examples of what could be wrong.

Activity 59: What is sexual health?

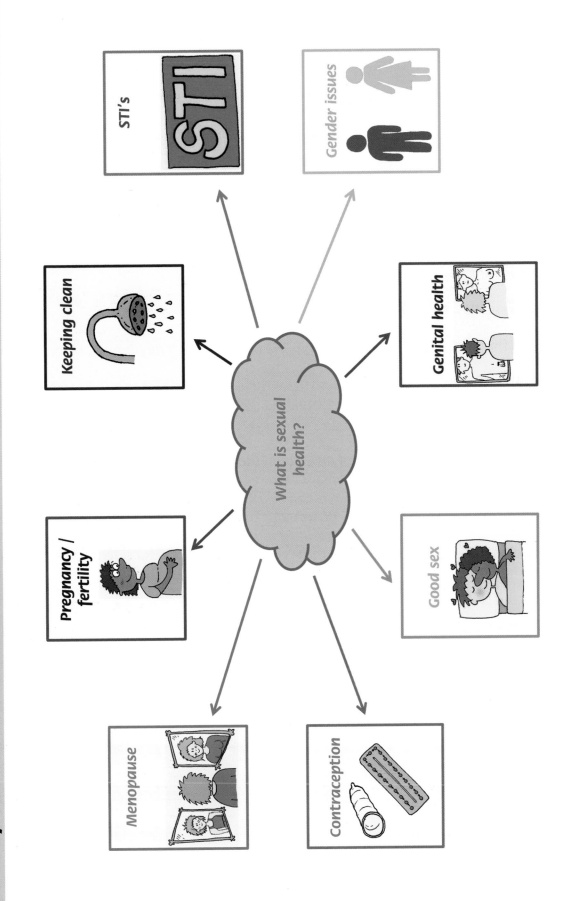

Activity 60: Speaking up for sexual health

Preparation

You will need to enlarge the ideas sheet to A3 for group work or print A4 copies if group members work individually.

If you will be using this more than once you may wish to print two copies, laminate one copy then cut out the different ideas on the other then laminate and Velcro™ these on.

Print a copy of the worksheet for each group member.

Instructions

- The group should sit around a table for this activity.

- Explain to the group that they will be doing the final activity today around sexual health.

- If you have attached Velcro™ to the ideas, take these off. Ask group members to take it in turns to think of ideas for what they could do if they needed support with their sexual health.

- Each time a group member thinks of an idea on the sheet, give them the corresponding idea card for them to stick on.

- Once all the ideas have been added, go through them one at a time and discuss.

- Group members should then complete their 'my plan' worksheet considering their top three ideas of things they should do if they needed support with sexual health.

Activity 60: Speaking up for sexual health

Name: ....

Date: ....

What could I do?

- Tell a friend
- Talk to someone you trust
- something else?
- Go to a sexual health clinic
- Look up information in a book
- Go to a walk in centre
- Look up information online
- Tell your partner
- Talk to your support worker
- Make a doctor's appointment

Activity 60: Speaking up for sexual health

Name: .... Date: ....

My Plan

If I need support with sexual health I could…

1.

2.

3.

Remember!

It's your body and your choice! Everyone has the right to good sexual health services. Keeping safe and healthy is very important. Don't be afraid to ask!

Speaking up for yourself – top tips!

- Say what you want
- Give a reason
- Use a calm voice
- Use good eye contact
- Sit up straight
- Be confident – you can do this!

Certificates

Preparation

Print out a certificate for each group member, add in their name and then sign at the bottom.

Laminate the certificates if possible.

Instructions

- Hand out a certificate to each group member, one at a time, with a round of applause.

- You may wish to say one thing each group member has done particularly well as part of the relationships course.

- You may then wish to play a few group games to celebrate.

Certificate of Achievement!

Awarded to

....

Congratulations

You have completed Talkabout Sex and Relationships!

Date..

Signed ....

Certificates

🧍 Forms

Contents	page

Forms

Session Evaluation

Group ....

Group members present ....

Date ....

Session number ....

	Plan	Evaluation
Starter activity		
Main activities		
Finishing activity		

Completed by .... Date ....

Forms	Parent/Carer Letter (Under 16)

Address

Date

Dear .... [Parent / Guardian]

As you may be aware, we spend a lot of time supporting students to develop their interaction, confidence and friendships skills.

This term, we will be beginning group work with a number of students around intimate relationships, including sexual education with a key focus of staying safe. Topics will include body awareness, an introduction to what sex means, the rules around it and keeping ourselves safe and healthy.

We would like to invite you to an information evening to discuss the details of what we will be covering in the groups and also answer any questions you may have [Optional].

If you would not like your child to be part of this group, please complete and return the slip below.

In the meantime, if you would like to discuss this further please do not hesitate to contact me.

Kind regards,

[Your name]

I do not want my child .... to complete the above relationships group work this term.

Signed .... Date...............................

Forms	Parent/Carer Letter (Over 16)

Address

Date

Dear .... [Parent / Guardian]

As you may be aware, we spend a lot of time supporting people to develop their interaction, confidence and friendships skills.

We will now be beginning group work around intimate relationships and sexual education with a key focus of staying safe. Topics will include; body awareness, an introduction to what sex means, the rules around it and keeping ourselves safe and healthy.

We would like to invite you to an information evening to discuss the details of what we will be covering in the groups and also answer any questions you may have [Optional].

In the meantime, if you would like to discuss this further please do not hesitate to contact me.

Kind regards,

[Your name]

👤 References and further reading

Brown, H. & Benson, S. (1995) *A Practical Guide to Working with People with Learning Disabilities: A Handbook for Care Assistants and Support Workers.* London, Hawker Publications Ltd.

Craft, M. & Craft, A. (1982) *Sex and the Mentally Handicapped: A Guide for Parents and Carers* (Revised Edition). London, Routledge and Kegan Ltd.

Craft, A. & Craft, M. (1983) *Sex Education & Counselling for Mentally Handicapped People.* Tunbridge Wells, Costello.

Cross, M. (1998) *Proud Child, Safer Child: A Handbook for Parents and Carers of Disabled Children.* London, The Women's Press Ltd.

Department of Education (2017) 'Press release: 'Schools to teach 21st century relationships and sex education'. [online] https://www.gov.uk/government/news/schools-to-teach-21st-century-relationships-and-sex-education [Accessed 23rd November 2017].

Fanstone, C. & Andrews, S. (2005) *Learning Disabilities, Sex and the Law: A Practical Guide.* London, FPA.

Firth, H. & Rapley, M. (1990) *From Acquaintance to Friendship: Issues for People with Learning Disabilities.* Kidderminster, BIMH Publications.

FPA (2008) 'Sexual Health Week 4–10 August 2008 – It's My Right!'. [online] https://www.fpa.org.uk/sexual-health-week/its-my-right [Accessed 23rd November 2017].

Grieve, A., McLaren, S., Lindsay, W. & Culling, E. (2009) 'Staff Attitudes towards the Sexuality of People with Learning Disabilities: A Comparison of Different Professional Groups and Residential Facilities', *British Journal of Learning Disabilities*, 37, 76–84.

Kelly, A. (2004) *TALKABOUT Relationships.* Bicester, Speechmark.

Kelly, A. (2011) *TALKABOUT for Children Developing Self-awareness and Self-esteem.* Milton Keynes, Speechmark.

Kelly, A. (2011) *TALKABOUT for Children Developing Social Skills.* Milton Keynes, Speechmark.

Kelly, A. (2013) *TALKABOUT for Children Developing Friendship Skills.* Milton Keynes, Speechmark.

Kelly, A. (2014) *TALKABOUT for Adults Developing Self-awareness and Self-esteem*. Milton Keynes, Speechmark.

Kelly, A. (2016) *TALKABOUT A Social Communication Skills Package* (2nd Edition). Milton Keynes, Speechmark.

Kelly, A. & Dennis, E. (2017) *TALKABOUT Sex & Relationships 1: A Programme to Develop Intimate Relationship Skills*. London, Routledge.

Kelly, A. & Sains, B. (2009) *TALKABOUT for Teenagers*. Bicester, Speechmark.

Kelly, A. & Sains, B. (2010) *TALKABOUT Assessment*. Bicester, Speechmark.

Maslow, A. (1962) *Toward a Psychology of Being* (2nd Edition). London, Van Nostrand Company Ltd.

McCarthy, M. (1999) *Sexuality and Women with Learning Disabilities*. London, Jessica Kingsley Publishers.

Rubin, K. (2002) *The Friendship Factor: Helping Our Children to Navigate Their Social World and Why it Matters for Their Success and Happiness*. New York, Penguin Books.

Sex Education Forum (2011) 'Teacher training model sustains improvement to school SRE'. [online] http://www.sexeducationforum.org.uk/resources/practice/sex-relationships-education/teacher-training-model-sustains-improvement-to-school-sre.aspx [Accessed 23rd November 2017].

The Independent (2017) 'Sex education to be made compulsory in all schools in England, government confirms'. [online] http://www.independent.co.uk/news/education/education-news/sex-relationships-education-made-compulsory-in-all-schools-england-justine-greening-government-a7605396.html [Accessed 23rd November 2017].

The Telegraph (2017) 'Sex education needs to be more graphic because teens are trying taboo practices, say experts'. [online]

http://www.telegraph.co.uk/science/2017/11/20/sex-education-needs-graphic-teens-trying-taboo-practices-say/ [Accessed 23rd November 2017].
Tindall, B. (2015) 'Decisions to safeguard adults with learning disabilities can make them less safe'. Community Care, April. [online] http://www.communitycare.co.uk/2015/04/21/decisions-safeguard-adults-learning-disabilities-can-make-less-safe/.

Westwood, J. & Mullan, B. (2007) 'Knowledge and Attitudes of Secondary School Teachers Regarding Sexual Health Education in England'. *Sex Education*, May, 143–159.

Wolfensberger, W. (1972) *The Principle of Normalization in Human Services.* Ontario, The National Institute on Mental Retardation.

Yacoub, E. & Hall, I. (2009) 'The Sexual Lives of Men with Mild Learning Disability: A Qualitative Study', *British Journal of Learning Disabilities*, 37, 5–11.

Index

Index	Page

Index / Page

Index | Page